W9-BXW-759

THE ULTIMATE
Tailgater's™
SEC
HANDBOOK

STEPHEN LINN

theultimatetailgater.com

[interactive blvd]™

An Interactive Blvd Book
interactiveblvd.com

The Globe Pequot Press

GUILFORD, CONNECTICUT

To buy books in quantity for corporate use
or incentives, call **(800) 962–0973**
or e-mail **premiums@GlobePequot.com.**

Copyright © 2007 by 4964 Productions, LLC.

An Interactive Blvd Book. Interactive Blvd is a division of 4964 Productions, LLC.
interactiveblvd.com.

All rights reserved. No part of this book may be reproduced or transmitted in any form by any means, electronic or mechanical, including photocopying and recording, or by any information storage and retrieval system, except as may be expressly permitted by the 1976 Copyright Act or by the publisher. Requests for permission should be made in writing to The Globe Pequot Press, P.O. Box 480, Guilford, Connecticut 06437.

This book is sold without warranties, express or implied, and the publisher and author disclaim any liability for injury, loss, or damage caused by the contents of this book.

All trademarks, service marks, and trade names referenced in this book are the property of their respective owners. All rights reserved.

Design by Karen Williams [Intudesign.net]

Photographs: Alabama: Barry Fikes, Arkansas: Spencer Tirey, Auburn: Todd Van Ernst, Florida: Jason Wise and Laurel Wise, Georgia: Radi Nabulsi, Kentucky: Brian Tietz. LSU: Patrick Dennis, Mississippi: Bruce Newman, Mississippi State: Thomas Wells, South Carolina: Brett Flashnick, Tennessee: Jason R. Davis, Vanderbilt: Ed Rode.

Special thanks to Barb Rishaw, Steve Ney, Ed Rode, Shanon Davis, Karen Williams, and Scott Adams for all of their help and support with this project.

Library of Congress Cataloging-in-Publication Data is on file.

ISBN 978-0-7627-4496-1

Manufactured in the United States of America

First Edition/First Printing

TABLE OF CONTENTS

THE SEC

If you're looking for tailgating country, you've found it. The Southeastern Conference is home to some of the most spirited and best-known tailgating in America . . . from Rocky Top to The Grove, with several stops in between. The SEC is also home to some of the most diverse tailgate menus of any conference; what's on the menu at LSU is a whole other world from what comes off the grill in South Carolina.

This is also the conference that hosts what's commonly acknowledged as the biggest tailgate party in the country (probably the world). It's in Jacksonville each year, the neutral field where Georgia plays Florida. It's called The World's Largest Outdoor Cocktail Party, and as many as 150,000 fans have packed the town to tailgate for several days (only 76,000 can fit inside Alltel Stadium). In 2006 the Florida and Georgia university presidents asked that the game officially be called the Georgia-Florida Game due to concern about the consumption of alcohol by college students. The city agreed. They'll probably be the only ones. The reality is fans will call the tailgating event The World's Largest Outdoor Cocktail Party for years to come—if not forever.

SEC HEISMAN TROPHY WINNERS	
1942	Frank Sinkwich, Georgia
1959	Billy Cannon, LSU
1966	Steve Spurrier, Florida
1971	Pat Sullivan, Auburn
1980	George Rogers, South Carolina
1982	Herschel Walker, Georgia
1985	Bo Jackson, Auburn
1996	Danny Wuerffel, Florida

SEC fans have had a lot to cheer about since the conference formed in 1932. That was the year 13 members of the Southern Conference—those located south and west of the Appalachian Mountains—bolted to form the Southeastern Conference. Ten of the founding 13 are still members of the SEC (Sewanee left in 1940 and is now a Division III school, Georgia Tech left in 1964 and after a couple of moves is now a member of the ACC, and Tulane left the SEC in 1966 and is now a member of C-USA).

In 1991 Alabama, Auburn, Florida, Georgia, Kentucky, LSU, Mississippi, Mississippi State, Tennessee, and Vanderbilt were joined by Arkansas (from the now defunct Southwest Conference) and South Carolina (from the independent football ranks, and the Metro Conference in other sports) to create the current SEC.

The following year, with the conference split into two divisions, the SEC was the first conference to hold a conference championship game (Alabama beat Florida 28–21).

SEC fans celebrate the conference's eight Heisman winners and the fact that nine of its current members have hoisted the national championship trophy since 1934 . . . several of those members a few times each.

VENUE AND PRICING GUIDES

For each city in the SEC, I've included a campus snapshot that includes a tailgating venue guide. That's what all the icons are; use the chart below to learn what you can and can't do outside the stadium. At the time this book was printed all of the information was correct; but things can change, so be sure to check the school's Web site or call ahead if you have any questions.

For restaurants and attractions in the area, I've included a pricing guide to help you manage your budget. A quick note about the suggestions for things like restaurants and hotels: as a rule, I haven't included chains in the list. I figure you can find a Denny's or Hilton on your own. I've included suggestions for places unique to the city that you won't find anywhere else.

 Decorations are allowed, excluding banners and signs that are advertising services or goods.

 Alcohol is permitted for those of legal drinking age.

 Grills or cookers are permitted for noncommercial use only.

 Parking is more than $50 per day for cars or larger vehicles.

 Parking is between $30 and $50 per day for cars or larger vehicles.

 Parking is no more than $30 per day for any vehicle.

 RVs may park overnight before or after the game.

 Number of hours you can tailgate before game. Times exceeding 4 hours are included in "4" icon.

 Number of hours you may remain after the event. Usually this includes tailgating, but read the entry to be sure.

 RVs, limos, and other oversized vehicles are allowed.

 Tents may be erected.

 Tables, chairs, and other tailgating furniture are allowed.

 Venue offers visible security presence in parking and tailgating areas.

 Venue offers at least one paved parking lot.

 Shuttle service is available from parking or tailgating areas to the event and back again.

Pricing Guide for Restaurants and Attractions

Restaurants (based on average entrée price):
$ $1–$19
$$ $20–$39
$$$ $40+

Attractions (based on average general admission price):
$ $1–$9
$$ $10–$19
$$$ $20+

ALABAMA

University of Alabama: 20,969 students
Tuscaloosa, AL: pop. 79,294
Bryant-Denny Stadium: seats 83,818
Colors: Crimson and White
Nickname: Crimson Tide
Mascot: Big Al
Phone: (205) 348-6113 Tide Pride, (205) 348-8391 parking services

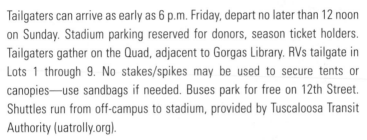

Tailgaters can arrive as early as 6 p.m. Friday, depart no later than 12 noon on Sunday. Stadium parking reserved for donors, season ticket holders. Tailgaters gather on the Quad, adjacent to Gorgas Library. RVs tailgate in Lots 1 through 9. No stakes/spikes may be used to secure tents or canopies—use sandbags if needed. Buses park for free on 12th Street. Shuttles run from off-campus to stadium, provided by Tuscaloosa Transit Authority (uatrolly.org).

Shuttle Info: Shuttles run from University Mall (10th Ave. across from Stadium), $10, and from downtown across from AmSouth Bank, $4.

Crimson Tide Media Partners: 99.5-FM WZRR, 690-AM WJOX, 94.1-FM WZBQ, 105.5-FM WRTR

The University of the State of Alabama, as it was first known, opened its doors in 1831 in Tuscaloosa. At the time the town was Alabama's capital (it moved to Montgomery in 1847) and where Congress had set aside land in the new Alabama Territory for a "seminary of learning."

Alabama opened as an academy-style institution emphasizing the classics and social and natural sciences. It was one of the first schools in the nation to offer engineering classes. But it was also a school in a state that still had much of its territory under the control of various Native American tribes and was without the educational infrastructure to adequately prepare students for university-level learning. Few students graduated; many more

ALMA MATER

Alabama, listen, Mother,
To our vows of love,
To thyself and to each other,
Faithful friends we'll prove.

Faithful, loyal, firm and true,
Heart bound to heart will beat.
Year by year, the ages through
Until in Heaven we meet.

College days are swiftly fleeting,
Soon we'll leave their halls
Ne'er to join another meeting
'Neath their hallowed walls.

Faithful, loyal, firm and true
Heart bound to heart will beat
Year by year, the ages through
Until in Heaven we meet.

So, farewell, dear Alma Mater
May thy name, we pray,
Be rev'renced ever, pure and
stainless
As it is today.

Faithful, loyal, firm and true
Heart bound to heart will beat
Year by year, the ages through
Until in Heaven we meet.

had discipline problems. While there were a number of strict rules in place for students, fights—often with knives and guns—were common. To instill more discipline on campus, in 1869, the school asked the state to make Alabama a military school. The state agreed.

Many cadets went on to serve as officers and to fight for the Confederate Army during the Civil War. Some historians feel that fact is the main reason Union forces burned most of the campus to the ground. Just seven buildings stood when the conflict ended. The school didn't reopen until 1871.

In the 1960s, Alabama was the scene of another battle—integration. Although Alabama first enrolled an African-American student in 1956 (and then expelled her three days later "for her own safety" after several threats), it was Gov. George Wallace blocking Foster Auditorium's front door in 1963 in an attempt to prevent two African-Americans from enrolling as students that made 'Bama a national focal point of race relations. Federal marshals and Attorney General Robert F. Kennedy convinced Wallace to stand aside, and the university was integrated.

It was between these events that Alabama's gridiron battles began, when a man named W. G. Little walked on campus "carrying his uniform and a great bag of enthusiasm" for football in 1892, as a 1926 student newspaper article put it. That

November, in Birmingham, W. G. and several other Alabama students challenged a hand-picked team of mostly Birmingham high school students and buried them 56–0. The next day (scheduling was a bit different then) the team played the Birmingham Athletic Club and lost 5–4 when the BAC kicked a 65-yard field goal to win. Football caught on, but in 1896 the school forbid teams from traveling off campus, so the next year there was just one game. The year after that the sport was abandoned. But that didn't last long; a student uproar reinstated the game in 1899, and one of the richest football traditions in America took root.

Alabama is where stars like Lee Roy Jordan, Ozzie Newsome, and Joe Namath played. But it is Paul "Bear" Bryant, who coached the team from 1958 to 1982 and won 6 national championships (the school has 11 championships in all), who is forever the face of 'Bama football.

Bryant arrived at Alabama after coaching stints at Maryland, Kentucky, and Texas A&M. He inherited a team that had won a combined total of four games the previous 3 years. He turned the team around right away. His first season the team went 5-4-1. The next year the Crimson Tide went to a bowl game. Two years after that, in 1961, Alabama went 11-0 and won the national championship.

When he retired, Bryant's record at Alabama was 232-46-9, and he had ascended to college football legend. In the state of Alabama, he was even more

than that. They thought so much of him that at the 1968 Democratic National Convention, he received 1 1/2 delegate votes for president of the United States, which was a surprise to him. No word as to whether it was a surprise to nominee Hubert Humphrey.

School Mascot

The Alabama football team has been called a variety of names, including the Varsity and the Crimson White, in reference to the school colors. But the first nickname that stuck was Thin Red Line, popularized by headline writers and used until 1906.

The next year Alabama was first tagged the Crimson Tide by the sports editor of the *Birmingham Age-Herald*, Hugh Roberts. Roberts used the phrase to describe the team that played far above expectations holding heavily favored Auburn to a 6–6 tie in a wet, muddy game. The *Birmingham News* sports editor picked up the term, and he is the one credited with turning it from a phrase into Alabama's nickname. Skip ahead to 1930, and Alabama's mascot is born: the elephant.

Another sports writer—this time Everett Strupper of the *Atlanta Journal*—wrote an article about the Alabama-Mississippi State game played that October and about the size and strength of the Crimson Tide players. "At the end of the quarter," he wrote, "the earth started to tremble, there was a distant rumble that continued to grow. Some excited fan in the stands bellowed, 'Hold your horses, the elephants are coming,' and out stamped this Alabama varsity." From then on, the elephant has been a part of Alabama football, although it was in the late 1970s when the mascot finally got a name; Big Al was the winning entry in a campus-wide contest.

Game-Day Traditions
The Million Dollar Band

Alabama takes pride in its history and tradition. There's the bonfire pep rally the night before each season's homecoming game. Homecoming day finds the annual parade run beside the Quad. Before every home game you hear the recorded voice of the legendary "Bear" Bryant echo through the stadium. And every 'Bama fan has a place in his or her heart for the scene of the players enjoying a victory cigar after defeating rival Tennessee. But perhaps the school's best-known tradition is its historic Million Dollar Band. Begun in 1914 as a military band, it has become one of the nation's most recognizable college bands. *Sports Illustrated* has listed the Million Dollar Band as one of the top three college bands in America, and the university claims the band has appeared on national television more than any other college band.

The name comes from the band's fund-raising prowess in 1922. Finances were tight, and the only way the band could make it to Georgia Tech for a game was by raising funds from merchants and anyone else who would help. They scraped together

Alabama Fight Song

"Yea, Alabama"

Yea, Alabama! Drown 'em Tide!
Every 'Bama man's behind you,
Hit your stride.
Go teach the Bulldogs to behave,
Send the Yellow Jackets to a watery grave.
And if a man starts to weaken,
That's a shame!
For Bama's pluck and grit have
Writ her name in Crimson flame.
Fight on, fight on, fight on men!
Remember the Rose Bowl, we'll win then.
So roll on to victory,
Hit your stride,
You're Dixie's football pride,
Crimson Tide, Roll Tide, Roll Tide!!!

enough to make the trip and play halftime at the game, which 'Bama lost 33–7.

An Atlanta sports writer asked Alabama alumnus W. C. "Champ" Pickens, "You don't have much of a team, what do you have at Alabama?" To which Pickens replied, "A Million Dollar Band." A tradition was born.

Visiting Alabama

Tuscaloosa may have started as the state capital, but it lost that title a long time ago (in 1846, to be exact) and is primarily a small college town with some great hole-in-the-wall places and good southern hospitality. The area does have a bit of German influence now, since DaimlerChrysler has a Mercedes-Benz plant here, along with the only Mercedes-Benz Museum in the world, outside of Germany (call (888) 286-8762 if you want to visit).

Where to Stay

❶ **Warner Lodge:** Located about 12 miles from downtown, on the shores of Lake Tuscaloosa, this hotel is about as far removed from your average chain-motel experience as champagne is from seltzer. The lobby resembles those hunting lodges built by turn-of-the-century industrial barons, and the lodge offers amenities like golf, tennis, swimming, and other fitness options. It's also attached to the Westervelt Warner Museum of American Art (*warnermuseum.org*), which houses one of the best collections of American Art you'll find anywhere. Football season rates run $165–$205. (*(205) 343-4215, warnerlodge.com*) ❷ **Oakmont Bed & Breakfast:** This B&B is about 30 miles south of Tuscaloosa, but a pretty straight shot into town. The Greek-Revival house was built in 1908, although it looks like a set piece from *Gone with the Wind*. There are four comfortable guest rooms, each with a private bath. Rooms run $100. (*(205) 372-2326, bbonline.com*) ❸ **Deerlick Creek Campground:** This is a good place to set up camp if you're traveling by RV. It's an Army Corps of Engineers campground located on Holt Lake, a few miles northeast of Tuscaloosa, with 46 sites available (40 have hookups). There are no sewer hookups, but they do have a dumping service. There's a two-night minimum stay. Rates $10–16. (*(205) 553-9373, sam.usace.army.mil/op/rec/war-tom/*) ❹ **Lake Lurleen State Park:** Another good RV park with 91 sites. All have water and electrical hookups; 35 have sewer hookups. Swimming, fishing, and boat launch are included in the camping fee (you'll need to supply the appropriate fishing and boating licenses). There's a two-night minimum stay during football season. Rates $16–20. (*(205) 339-1558, alapark.com*)

Where to Eat

TAILGATE SUPPLIES: ❶ **Manna Grocery & Deli:** Founded in 1980 as a health-oriented grocery, Manna first offered customers whole, unrefined, and organic foods and supplements. Almost 30 years later, the store now features a deli with freshly made soups and sandwiches, and more than 10,000 different items on the shelves. (*(205) 752-9955, mannagrocery.com*)

SPORTS BARS: ❷ **Bob Baumhower's Wings Sports Grille:** Founded in 1981 by 'Bama Alum and six-time Miami Dolphins All-Pro Bob Baumhower, this location is one of eight across Alabama. Inside, it's got everything a good sports bar should have—plenty of cool sports memorabilia, enough TVs to keep your eyes busy, and an affordable, extensive menu of chicken, fish, beef, and pork dishes. (*$, (205) 556-5658, wingssportsgrille.com*) ❸ **Buffalo Phil's:** This is another favorite spot on game day, packed with 'Bama fans watching one of the seven TVs on the wall—including a 50-inch plasma TV over the bar—and scarfing down an endless selection of wings and beer (they have other stuff, too). (*$, (205) 758-3318, buffalophils.com*) ❹ **The Hound's Tooth:** Picked as the #1 college sports bar in America by *Sports Illustrated* in 2005, it's got loads of TVs (even in the bathrooms), four pool tables, a dart board, and a Golden Tee machine. It also opens at 8 a.m. on football Saturdays. Images of "Bear" Bryant cover the walls. (*$, (205) 752-8444, houndstoothsportsbar.com*)

RESTAURANTS: ❺ **BottomFeeders:** It's barely larger than a double-wide trailer with florescent lighting, Formica tables, and knick-knacks of sunflowers and pigs, but locals will tell you this place is one reason many consider Tuscaloosa the capital of Alabama barbecue. The menu has everything from ribs to catfish. No alcohol is served. (*$, (205) 758-7447, BottomFeedersBBQ.com*) ❻ **City Café:** This is where to go for good no frills, Southern home-cooking. The line for breakfast starts forming long before sunrise, and again for lunch. Why? Because they have homemade Southern favorites served up by waitresses who've worked there since Moses was a baby (well, maybe not *that* long). (*$, (205) 758-9171, tuscaloosarestaurant.com*) ❼ **Cypress Inn:** Inside this charming restaurant, you'll find a nautical-themed space with high ceilings, warm candlelight, and the Black Warrior River flowing by. Cypress Inn specializes in American cuisine with an emphasis on seafood. Reservations are not accepted on weekends. (*$, (205) 345-6963, cypressinnrestaurant.com*) ❽ **DePalma's Italian Café:** Located in downtown Tuscaloosa, DePalma's seduces residents and visitors alike with a combination of good food, reasonable prices, and pleasantly funky atmosphere. The extensive menu ranges from inexpensive standards to more expensive specialties. (*$–$$, (205) 759-1879, tuscaloosa restaurant.com*)

Daytime Fun

❶ **The Aliceville Museum:** This museum collects, preserves, and displays artifacts from Camp Aliceville, a WWII German POW

camp. You'll see letters, artwork, uniforms, photos, and books from more than 6,000 German prisoners of war housed there during 1942 to 1945. (*$, (205) 373-2363, alicevillemuseum.pickens.net*) ❷ **Bama Belle Riverboat:** This modern-day replica of the paddlewheel riverboats that cruised the nation's river ways in the early 1900s offers leisurely sightseeing and dinner cruises along the Black Warrior River. Sightseeing trips are fairly inexpensive ($9 for an adult). Every Saturday evening the riverboat hosts a dinner cruise with a menu that wouldn't be out of place in an upscale restaurant. Dinner requires a reservation and more money ($42 for an adult). (*$–$$$, (205) 339-1108, bamabelle.com*) ❸ **Moundville Archaeological Park:** This is a great place to spend a few hours learning about America's first urbanites, the Mississippian Native Americans. About 800 years ago, these people had a serious civilization going—they had organized villages and cities, temples, trading routes, and farmland throughout the midsection of North America. Moundville is one of the biggest and best preserved. Think of it as the Big Apple of the 14th century. (*$, (205) 371-2234, moundville.ua.edu*) ❹ **The Paul W. Bryant Museum:** That's Bryant, as in "Bear," so this is holy ground for Crimson Tide fans. You can't claim to have actually visited Tuscaloosa for a game without paying a visit to this shrine. The museum showcases more than 100 years of Alabama football history. You'll need to schedule about an hour to see everything (or longer, if you want to linger over your favorite years). (*$, (866) 772-BEAR, bryant.ua.edu*)

❺ **Tuscaloosa Walking Tour:** At 2 1/4 miles, it's an easy amble through the heart of downtown Tuscaloosa. The tour starts at Jemison Mansion/Tuscaloosa Visitors Center and covers Greensboro Ave. and University Blvd. Just follow the sidewalk markers, and stroll past unique architecture, cool shops, fine art galleries, and plenty of pit stops for great food. (*Free, tcvb.org*)

Nighttime Fun

❶ **4th and 23rd:** This is a renovated warehouse with high ceilings, a long wooden bar, pool tables, and couches on the balcony for people-watching and for just looking cool. The club was originally known for jazz and blues, but now books all sorts of acts. A DJ spins tunes when there's no band. (*$, (205) 248-0255, 4thand23rd.net*) ❷ **Harry's Bar:** It's a scruffy, dirty, occasionally rough, little dive bar opened in 1972 by UA football star Harry Hammond (hence the name). Harry's ceiling panels are covered with the names of students, residents, and organizations that have visited Harry's over the years. Supposedly, somewhere in that tangle of names is a young Joe Namath's signature. (*$,

(205) 758-9332) ❸ **Jupiter Bar and Grill:** This place has great live music and books some national-level bands, like Everclear and the Velcro Pygmies. You'll also find a wide range of genres, from alternative rock and Americana to country and rap. The Jupiter's menu is better than most bars, with entrée salads, pasta dishes, and prime rib. *($, (205) 248-6611, jupiteronthestrip.com)*

Shopping

❶ **Bama Bean:** It's part coffee house, part coffee supplier, part gift shop, and all 'Bama football. While they have a nice little menu, it's the unique 'Bama memorabilia you'll wander in for. Alongside the usual gift items, you'll find Alabama Easter baskets and hand-decorated eggs, as well as limited-edition serigraph prints. *((205) 758-1100, bamabean.com)* ❷ **Downtown Trading Company:** Located in Tuscaloosa's historic downtown, this fun shop has a little bit of everything for everybody. It used to be strictly a cigar store, and you'll still find a good selection of humidors and aromatic tobacco products. But the Trading Company now offers exotic home décor, incense, oils and candles, specialty bath products, "tribal" jewelry, and consignment art. *((888) 628-8312, downtowntradingcompany.com)* ❸ **The Trunk:** If you want your official Alabama gear, go straight to The Trunk, located in the shadow of the Bryant-Denny Stadium. Here in this Alabama-alumni-owned store, you'll find all things 'Bama—from children's bloomers to steak sauce to a bronze or pewter bust of "Bear" Bryant. *((800) HEYBAMA, heybama.com)*

ARKANSAS

University of Arkansas: 16,035 students
Fayetteville, AR: pop. 67,020
Donald W. Reynolds Stadium: seats 72,000
Colors: Cardinal and White
Nickname: Razorbacks
Mascot: Tusk I (live), Big Red, Sue E, and
Pork Chop (costumed), Boss Hog (inflatable)
Phone: (479) 575-4412

RVs arrive as early as Wednesday before the game and park at Road Hog Park at Razorback Road & 15th, $20–30 per day. Cars park for free in any non-reserved lot and in grassy areas adjacent to lots, as well as at the Gardens. Keep tailgating within your parking space. Don't use tent spikes. Tailgating allowed from 7 a.m. to 9 p.m.

Shuttle Info: Free shuttles available from public parking at Baum Stadium and Baldwin Piano to a Bud Walton Arena drop-off before the game (buses will return to those areas after the game). Shuttles start 4 hours before kickoff, running until all fans are returned to their vehicles.

Razorbacks Media Partners: 103.7-FM KABZ, 920-AM, 102.9-FM KARN

Arkansas Industrial University opened to students in 1871 (it changed its name to the University of Arkansas in 1899). Rising from the heart of the campus in 1875 was the original administration and instructional building, known as Old Main. It's built in the Second Empire style and is listed on the National Register of Historic Places. It is also, the story goes, a standing monument to the legacy of the Civil War, as well as a reminder to keep an eye on your contractors.

Old Main has two towers. When architects designed the building, the plans called for the south tower to be taller than the north tower. It was a

post-Civil War salute to the South. But the crews actually building the towers were Northern contractors, and as they erected Old Main they made a slight change to the plans. It wasn't until Old Main was finished that anyone realized they had built the North tower taller than the South.

The lawn at Old Main is also a popular spot on campus. It serves as a state arboretum of sorts, where you can find one of every type of tree that grows anywhere in the state.

In the years after the Old Main incident, many of the tensions of the Civil War gradually passed, and in 1948, the University of Arkansas was the first major southern public school to admit an African-American student without litigation. His name was Silas Hunt, and he enrolled in the law school.

Football came to Fayetteville in 1894. The first team was known as the Arkansas Cardinals, named for the school color chosen earlier that year. The other color finalist, by the way, was heliotrope, a shade of purple.

The Cardinals' first season included two wins against Fort Smith High School and a 54–0 loss to the Texas Longhorns. But the team's fortunes changed during the next few seasons, and in 1909, Arkansas went 7-0, and the coach said his team played "like a wild band of razorback hogs." That's all it took. The name became so popular that in 1910 Arkansas became the Razorbacks, aka the Hogs. About 10 years later "Woo, Pig! Sooie!" was first heard. More on that in a bit.

Arkansas was a charter member of the Southwest Conference in 1914, where it played until the SWC fell apart in 1991. (That's when the Hogs moved to the SEC.) The team had several very successful seasons under coaches Frank Broyles, Lou Holtz, and Ken Hatfield, and won 13 SWC championships—including in 1964 when it won the national championship. Sort of.

That year at least eight organizations named a national champion. AP and UPI, the two major polls whose 1964 champion you find in most record books, named Alabama the national champion that year. The only problem is they awarded the title before the bowl games were played. Alabama played in the Orange Bowl that year, but didn't play well; the Crimson Tide lost to Texas 21–17. That left Arkansas as the only undefeated team that season at 11-0 (the Hogs beat Nebraska in the Cotton Bowl). While folks like the Billingsley Report, the Football Writers Association, and the Helms Athletic Foundation named Arkansas national champion, Alabama got to keep the official title. The next year both AP and UPI changed their rules and began wait-ing until after bowl season to name their champions.

As an SEC team, Arkansas hasn't had simi-larly successful teams. The Hogs have played in a couple of SEC championship games, but the Razorbacks haven't won the crown. They did, however, take the SEC West title in 2006. Four Arkansas players from the SEC era have been selected in the first round of the NFL draft: Henry Ford (1994), Shawn Andrews and Ahmad Carroll (2004), and Matt Jones (2005).

School Mascot

There's only one major athletic program in the country that calls its team a porcine nickname. This is it. A razorback is a feral pig; it became an athletic nickname in 1910 and it—or the more colloquial Hogs—is what the U of A calls its all-male sports teams. The women's teams are the Lady Razorbacks.

The wild razorbacks that called Arkansas home in the 1900s were not the cute, cuddly pigs of your childhood, or the porkers at the county fair. They were of the wild boar variety, untamed, ill-tempered, and prone to fight. When they did, they usually won.

It was these animals that Coach Hugo Bezdek spoke of when he uttered the comparison that became the school's moniker. Now, other than on the football field, the only wild razorbacks roam the Outback of Australia. The one that roams the sidelines in Fayetteville is Tusk I, a Russian boar that resembles a razorback.

The costumed ones roaming the stands don't look anything like a real razorback, and they're named Big Red and Sue E. The little mascot is Pork Chop. The 9-foot-tall inflatable one is Boss Hog. Certainly not names the original razorbacks would have taken a liking to, but they are cuter.

Game-Day Traditions
Running Through the "A"

As the 280-member Razorback Marching Band winds up its pregame routine before home games, the band marches the length of the field, with the crowd rising to its feet cheering, stops at the end zone in front of the Arkansas locker room, and forms a huge "A." After a few bars the team, led by its head coach, sprints through the "A" to the home sideline. They've been "running through the "A" for about a half-century in Fayetteville, and players who have long since retired to the stands on game day still talk about the chills they get watching the "A" form on the field.

The Lids

The Green Bay Packers have their Cheeseheads; the Arkansas Razorbacks have their Lids, aka "Hog Hats." The Hog Hats date back to the 1964 national championship season (see page 23 for more on that), and these red plastic hats, molded into the shape of a running Razorback, have become one of the

Arkansas Fight Song

Hit that line! Hit that line! Keep on going,

Move that ball right down the field!

Give a cheer. Rah! Rah! Never fear. Rah! Rah!

Arkansas will never yield!

On your toes, Razorbacks, to the finish,

Carry on with all your might!

For it's A-A-A-R-K-A-N-S-A-S for Arkansas!

Fight! Fight! Fi-i-i-ght!

most recognized team paraphernalia in sports.

Calling Those Hogs

It was during the 1920s—exactly when no one is sure—that Arkansas fans first "called the Hogs" during a game. Since then, this rallying cry of Razorback fans has become a game-day tradition and instantly recognizable as an Arkansas original. It goes like this:

> "Wooooooooooo, Pig! Sooie!
> "Wooooooooooo, Pig! Sooie!
> "Wooooooooooo, Pig! Sooie!
> Razorbacks!"

The words are simple enough, but getting the gestures and cadence down takes practice. You begin with your hands raised high, fingers waving as the volume of the "Wooooooooooo" gets louder and louder. Your arms come down when you say "Pig" and go back up on "Sooie!" Practice a few times at home before you try it at the game. Trust me.

Visiting Arkansas

Fayetteville is a pretty typical college town—although one that has seen its natives and residents become presidents (Bill Clinton), star athletes (golfer John Daly), and corporate titans (Wal-Mart cofounder Bud Walton). Often finding itself on lists of the best places to live in America, Fayetteville is a small town with a comfortable pace of life and a lot of outdoor recreational activities.

Where to Stay

❶ **Deepwood House:** This rustic home, constructed primarily of cut stone, cedar, and glass, seems to melt into the surrounding maple forest. Built in the early 1960s by a professor of architecture, this large house has three guest-rooms, including a master bedroom. Deep-wood can accommodate up to six people and is used as a guesthouse, instead of a bed and breakfast. Guests are usually responsible for their own meals, but arrangements can be made with prior notice. Rates are calculated on a sliding scale depending on length of stay and number of guests in your group. The best rate: 3–6 people, staying two nights, pay $225 per night for the whole house. (*(479) 571-3224, deepwoodhouse.com*) ❷ **Devil's Den State Park:** This state park is about 20 miles south of Fayetteville and has 48 sites. Unlike many state parks this one offers a variety of utility hookups, though no TV, phone, or Internet connections. The

ALMA MATER

Pure as the dawn on the brow of thy beauty
Watches thy soul from the mountains of God
Over the Fates of thy children departed
Far from the land where their footsteps have trod.
Beacon of hope in the ways dreary lighted;
Pride of our hearts that are loyal and true;
From those who adore unto one who adores us—
Mother of Mothers, we sing unto you.

We, with our faces turned high to the Eastward,
Proud of our place in the vanguard of Truth,
Will sing unto thee a new song of thanksgiving—
Honor to God and the Springtime of Youth.
Shout of the victor or tear of the vanquished;
Sunshine or tempest thy heart is e'er true;
Pride of the Hills and the white-laden Lowlands—
Mother of Mothers, we kneel unto you.

Ever the Legions of Sin will assail us,
Ever the Battle in Cities afar;
Still in the depths will thy Spirit eternal
Beckon us on like a piloting Star.
Down in dim years do thy dead children call thee,
Wafted to Sleep while the Springtime was new;
We, of the Present, thy hope of the Future—
Mother of Mothers, we pray unto you.

campground has paved roads and sites, but some roads can be rather narrow and twisty. The park recommends big-rigs take exit 53 at State Rte. 170 at West Fork to enter safely. Sites run $17–$29. (*(479) 761-3325, arkansasstateparks.com*)   ❸ **Inn at Carnall Hall:** This 50-room inn on the university's campus looks and feels more like a boutique hotel than campus lodgings. The hotel restaurant serves nouvelle dishes like a foie gras appetizer, and entrées like marinated duck breast with white sausage and butternut squash purée. Bet they don't get that in the dorms. Rooms run $132–$280 during football game weekends. (*(800) 295-9118, innatcarnallhall.com*)   ❹ **Mount Sequoyah Conference and Retreat Center:** Located atop Mt. Sequoyah, overlooking the Ozark Mountains and just minutes away from the stadium, this facility has rooms available for "personal retreats," as well as for larger groups. Reservations are essential, and meals can be provided by prior arrangement. Rooms run $75 on football weekends. (*(800) 760-8126, mountsequoyah.org*)   ❺ **Stay-Inn-Style:** This craftsman-style bungalow has six guestrooms with private baths, furnished with an eclectic mix of American antiques and some vivid colors. Most also have Jacuzzis and wood burning fireplaces. Rooms run $95–$115. No pets or young children. (*(800) 881-5668, stayinnstyle.com*)

❻ **Wanderlust RV Park:** In Eureka Springs, about 45 minutes northeast of Fayetteville, this park offers 90 sites with full utility hookups. Wireless and modem Internet connections are available, though phone and cable TV are not. The park has big-rig and pull-through access, is family-friendly, and allows pets. Sites cost $26. Cabins are also available for $65–$150. (*(800) 253-7385, wanderlust-rvpark.com*)

Where to Eat

TAILGATE SUPPLIES: ❶ **Fayetteville Farmers' Market:** This open-air food market runs from April until the middle of November on Saturdays. Merchants set up in Town Center Plaza, adjoining Fayetteville's town square. In addition to fresh, seasonal fruits and vegetables, you'll find honey, goat cheese, lamb, eggs, and mushrooms. (*(501) 575-1875, fayettevillefarmersmarket.org*) ❷ **Ozark Natural Foods:** This is a consumer-owned retail grocery store that offers a wide variety of whole and organic foods. This co-op is no little hole-in-the-wall, either. It's a large store with a good selection of produce, meat, and poultry, plus everything from frozen food to toilet paper. (*(479) 521-7558, ozarknaturalfoods.com*)

SPORTS BARS: ❸ **Cool Water Pub:** This relaxed sports pub is tucked inside the Cool Water Café (another place worth visiting). You'll find TVs sprinkled throughout the pub, billiards room, and cigar lounge, including a 9-foot projection screen TV. The crowd at Cool Water is a little older but just as fanatic. (*$, (479) 571-3636, coolwater cafe.com*) ❹ **Grub's Bar & Grill:** Grub's is a noisy, lively bar with a classic pub grub menu and 15 TVs, including a 10-foot giant screen. The 7,000-square-foot bar is lavishly covered with Razorbacks sports memorabilia and hoods from NASCAR race cars dangling from the ceiling. Upstairs is Grub's mezzanine with a second bar, a pool table, and a lounge. On football weekends Grub's features live music onstage. (*$, (479) 973-4782, grubsbar.net*) ❺ **On the Mark Sports Bar & Grill:** With more than 45 TVs, these guys are serious about sports. They're also serious about having a good time. On the Mark collects and displays all kinds of sports stuff, from the Razorbacks to NFL teams, NASCAR, even horse racing memorabilia. This local hangout also offers video games, shuffleboard, foosball, and trivia. (*$, (479) 575-0123*)

RESTAURANTS: ❻ **Bordinos:** The 2005 *Fayetteville Free Weekly Reader*'s Choice Awards named Bordinos "Best Atmosphere," "Most Romantic," "Best Special Occasion," "Best Wine List," and "Best Overall Restaurant." They're doing something right. The menu showcases Northern Italian cuisine, with some modern reinterpretations thrown in. Entrée prices vary widely—as little as $8.25 for penne pasta in a spicy tomato sauce to $35.50 for the lamb chops. (*$–$$, (479) 527-6795, bordinos.com*) ❼ **Brioso Brazil:** They have only one item on the menu, but it's a doozey—basically a gaucho-style, all-you-can-eat feast of meats, vegetables, and side dishes. Dinner includes soup, a salad buffet, lamb, linguica sausage, pork loin and ribs, steaks, chicken, and more. The meats are served tableside until you beg them to stop. (*$$, (479) 254-9933, briosobrazil.com*) ❽ **Hugo's:** It's a local institution, and it's easy to see why. This tiny bistro, located just off the town square, serves the best burgers in Fayetteville. They've been winning awards for them since 1977. The bistro's interior is filled with a vast collection of eclectic memorabilia. (*$, (479) 521-7585*)

Daytime Fun

❶ **Arkansas Air Museum:** From racing planes of the 1920s to navy carrier fighters, the museum walks visitors through Arkansas aviation history. The all-wood hangar that houses the planes, interactive exhibits, and memorabilia was the former headquarters for one of the U.S. aviator training posts during World War II. (*$, (479) 521-4947, arkairmuseum.org*)

❷ **Devil's Den State Park:** You'll see some of Arkansas's most spectacular scenery here, with deep crevices, mysterious caves, and striking bluff overlooks. This 2,000-acre park

provides a variety of hiking and multiuse trails, mountain biking, an 8-acre lake, rustic cabins, and caves of sandstone and limestone to explore—and you can rent the stuff you need to enjoy it all. Day visitors pay no fee to hike trails. There are varying charges for overnight camping, equipment or group facility rentals, and swimming pool use. (*Free–$$$, (479) 761-3325, arkansasstateparks.com*)

❸ **Washington-Willow Walking Tour:** Self-guided walking tours of the Washington/Willow Historic District begin at **Headquarters House** and wind through this beautiful neighborhood peppered with Victorian homes. While most are private residences, Headquarters House is open to the public and is an entertaining tour. Other tours, tailored to your tastes, can be arranged by calling the Washington County Historical Society. (*$–$$$, (479) 521-2970, washcohistoricalsociety.org*)

Nighttime Fun

❶ **The Common Grounds:** It's a favorite hangout for Fayetteville's 20- and 30-somethings. What started off as a little coffee house is now a happening joint with a full-service restaurant, bar, and a two-level deck. Located just down the hill from the university, the Grounds showcases paintings by local artists, frequently features live music, and has a pretty fresh menu. It's nighttime fun, but they serve breakfast too. (*$, (479) 442-3515, commongroundsar.com*) ❷ **Dickson Street:** Dickson Street runs through downtown Fayetteville and is home to the town's most active nightlife. Walk along the street and you'll find various clubs, bars, and restaurants to keep you occupied into the night. ❸ **JR's Dickson Theater:** This popular dance club offers a variety of entertainment options—from dance parties to film screenings and everything in between. The place starts shaking around 9 p.m. JR's also hosts an impressive lineup of national and regional music acts, so check their Web site to see who's playing. (*$–$$, (479) 575-0500, liveatjrs.com/dicksontheater*)

Shopping

❶ **Dickson Street:** If you want to go shopping in Fayetteville without going to a mall, this is a good place to start. Dickson Street's coffee shops, restaurants, and independent stores make it a good location for wandering, shopping, and people watching. Among the highlights is **Ebeez**, whose owner is married to a former Razorbacks player and stocks Hogs and Greek items. (*(479) 521-4995, ebeezonline.com*) **Collier Drug Store** (this is the original) is a throwback to an

earlier era with a restored Art Deco exterior and chrome lunch counter, stocking everything from prescription drugs to fresh flowers. (*(479) 442-6262, collierdrug.com*) ❷ **Hog Heaven:** The official team store, open daily in the Bud Walton Arena, carries a staggering inventory of Razorback items, and all profits go to the Men's Athletic Department. But that just makes this a store. What makes it Hog Heaven is that they sell game-used helmets, jerseys, footballs (some autographed), and other player-used and worn gear. (*(479) 575-3815, hogwired.com*)

AUBURN

Auburn University: 22,928 students
Auburn, AL: pop. 49,928
Jordan Hare Stadium: seats 87,451
Colors: Burnt Orange and Navy Blue
Nickname: Tigers
Mascot: Tiger (live), Aubie (costumed)
Phone: (800) AUB-1957

RVs can arrive as early as 4 p.m. Wednesday, first-come, first-served, park in grass lots on corner of Donahue Drive and Lem Morrison Drive. Parking is free. Tailgating allowed all day game day in any non-reserved lot and in core of campus. No amplified sound systems, no tent stakes longer than 12 inches. No grilling on parking decks. Grills must be 50' away from ANY campus structure.

Shuttle Info: All parking within easy walking distance. No shuttles needed.

Tigers Media Partner: 97.7-FM WKKR

Auburn University was chartered as East Alabama Male College in 1856, under the oversight of the Methodist Church. The first students began classes in 1859; there were 80 of them. But before long the Civil War would shutter the school as most of the students and faculty left to enlist. The campus was used as a training ground for the Confederate Army, and Old Main—the first and primary building on campus for classes—became a Confederate hospital. (Later, in 1887, Old Main was destroyed by fire.)

The school reopened in 1866 and became a state school in 1872, mostly for financial reasons, and that meant a new name: Agricultural and Mechanical College of Alabama. (The name changed again in 1899 to Alabama Polytechnic Institute, and then in 1960 it became Auburn University.)

In 1892 there were two firsts at the school: the first women were enrolled as students, and the first football game was played in Atlanta's Piedmont Park against Georgia. The Tigers won that game, which launched the oldest football rivalry in the South. In the decades since then, of course, Auburn's become one of America's premier programs, having gone undefeated, won conference championships, and won the national championship. The Tigers have played in more than 30 bowl games, but its first bowl appearance was a notable one.

It was in 1937 against Villanova in the Bacardi Bowl in Havana, Cuba. This was the first time two American universities played against each other on foreign soil. The game was almost cancelled when Cuban leader Fulgencio Batista (who was later overthrown by Fidel Castro) didn't find his picture in the game program. A quick reprint and the game was saved. Auburn's first bowl game ended in a 7–7 tie.

Over the years Auburn has produced some of the sport's best players, including Pat Sullivan and Bo Jackson, who both won Heisman Trophies, in 1971 and 1985,

respectively. And the trophy's namesake, John Heisman, coached here from 1895 to 1899.

School Mascot

Okay, let me clear up something that's confused fans, broadcasters, and others for years. Auburn's nickname is the Tigers. War Eagle is the school's battle cry. They are not interchangeable, and War Eagle VI, the school's eagle symbol/mascot, is even named "Tiger."

Now that we're clear, let's talk about where that name came from. After all, not a lot of tigers roam Alabama. The nickname comes from a line in Oliver

Goldsmith's 1770 poem "The Deserted Village." The line of inspiration is "where crouching tigers wait their hapless prey."

It was about two centuries later when Aubie, the costumed tiger you see on the sidelines, was born. Well, *sewn*.

Aubie began as a cartoon character on a football program cover in 1959, sketched by *Birmingham Post-Herald* artist Phil Neel. Over time Aubie transformed, standing upright in 1962, and wearing clothes in 1963 (a straw hat and blue tie). The costumed Aubie first took the field in 1979.

Game-Day Traditions
The Tiger Walk

I know scores of schools have a walk of some sort, but by all accounts they're copying Auburn.

The Tiger Walk began in the early 1960s when Auburn players would walk to the stadium from Sewell Hall. Thousands of fans would line Donahue Drive to cheer them on. Since then the crowds have gotten bigger (20,000 lined the streets before a 1989 Alabama game), and the tradition has even begun to spread to some road games.

Auburn Fight Song

"War Eagle"

War . . . Eagle, fly down the field,
Ever to conquer, never to yield.
War . . . Eagle fearless and true.
Fight on, you orange and blue.
Go! Go! Go!
On to vic'try, strike up the band,
Give 'em hell, give 'em hell.
Stand up and yell, hey!
War . . . Eagle, win for Auburn,
Power of Dixie Land!

The Entrance

I'm not sure you can call it a tradition yet—they started in 2000—but the Tigers now take the field from the middle of the south end zone through a cloud of smoke.

Toomer's Corner

When the Tigers win, you want to be the guy selling toilet paper.

Toomer's Corner is in the center of town and where fans gather after football victories to "roll the streets"—and anything else they can find—with toilet paper. Within a few hours it looks like a snow storm fell on the city. And your parents told you "papering" your friends' houses in high school wouldn't teach you any usable skills.

Visiting Auburn

Oliver Goldsmith didn't just give a school a nickname; he also gave a city its nickname. Auburn is often called The Loveliest Village on the Plains, which, like the tigers line that nicknamed Auburn University, comes from his 1770 poem "The Deserted Village." While Auburn may be a small college town, it is the fastest growing city in Alabama and in the top 20 nationally, due in part to the quality of its school system.

Where to Stay

❶ **Auburn Cottage:** This secluded, two-room cottage is 4 1/2 miles from Toomer's Corner, on a hill overlooking Saugahatchee Creek's whitewater rapids. The cottage has about 1,130 square feet with a large bathroom, a living area with television, a full kitchen, a dining area, and a large outdoor deck. Five people can sleep comfortably here with a queen-size bed, a queen-size sleeper sofa, and a rollaway bed. There is a two-night minimum stay. Rates for a two-night stay run from $400 to $600, depending on the game. Remember, rates are for both nights total, not per night. Tax not included. (*(334) 821-0091*) ❷ **Auburn's Game-day Center:** Why get just a room when you can rent an entire furnished condo? The Center has 23 rather nifty condos just off campus, with Tiger-themed furnishings and sufficient elbow

---

ALMA MATER

On the rolling plains of Dixie
'Neath its sun-kissed sky,
Proudly stands, our Alma Mater
Banners high.
To thy name we'll sing thy praise,
From hearts that love so true,
And pledge to thee our
Loyalty the ages through.

We hail thee, Auburn, and we vow
To work for thy just fame,
And hold in memory as we do now
Thy cherished name.

Hear thy student voices swelling,
Echoes strong and clear,
Adding laurels to thy fame
Enshrined so dear.
From thy hallowed halls we'll part,
And bid thee sad adieu;
Thy sacred trust we'll bear with us
The ages through.

We hail thee, Auburn, and we vow
To work for thy just fame,
And hold in memory as we do now
Thy cherished name.

room for you and a few friends to spread out and get comfortable. (*(800) 693-8204*) ❸ **Crenshaw House Bed & Breakfast:** Located just three blocks from the university, this late Victorian comes with 12-foot vaulted ceilings and heart pine floors. It offers three large guest rooms and one suite, all furnished in period-style antiques. While the décor might be Victorian, the amenities are 21st century. Rooms run $60–$100. The suite is priced $100–$125. (*(334) 821-1131, auburnalabamalodging.com*) ❹ **Heritage House Bed & Breakfast:** About 10 miles down the road in neighboring Opelika, this impressive Greek Revival mansion offers five guestrooms. Each comes with a television, a telephone, wireless Internet access, and a private bath. Well-behaved children 10 years and up are welcome, but pets (no matter how well-behaved) are not. Rates during football weekends are $295 for a two-day stay, and it's popular; you should try to book at least 6 months in advance. (*(334) 705-0485, opelikaheritagehouse.com*) ❺ **The Hotel at Auburn University and Dixon Conference Center:** This hotel has 243 nicely furnished guestrooms, plus three suites, located right on the university's campus. It comes with the amenities you'd expect in a hotel catering to business travelers, plus an on-site restaurant called **Ariccia** (after Auburn's international campus in Ariccia, Italy). Rooms usually run $99–$119. (*(800) 228-2876, auhcc.com*) ❻ **Leisure Time Campground:** Just 6 miles from the university, this RV campground has full hookups on all its 60 sites. It also offers cable TV, a dump station, and modem hookups, but no telephone or wireless Internet connections. It's best to arrive during daylight hours: check-in is frequently done on the honor system, and finding your space after dark, unaided, can be a pain. Spaces run $20. (*(334) 821-2267*)

Where to Eat

TAILGATE SUPPLIES: ❶ **Brunos:** You may pay a bit more, but this regional supermarket offers superior meats, seafood, produce (including organic), and extras like made-to-order sushi. (*(334) 466-8847*)

SPORTS BARS: ❷ **The Buffalo Connection Sports Grill:** Co-owned by ex-Auburn football star Byron Franklin, this is a fun place for sports fans. The walls are festooned with old sports memorabilia (especially football), while several televisions are strategically placed around the restaurant, including a (very) big-

screen in the middle. A children's menu is available. (*$, (334) 821-2700, buffcon.net*) ❸ **The Tiger's Den Tavern & Grill:** It has 28 TVs, including one in the women's restroom. The interior is a mix of blonde wood and Auburn orange. You'll also find live music, trivia contests, and karaoke, depending on the night you drop in. (*$, (334) 502-2491*)

RESTAURANTS: ❹ **The Creole and Seafood Shack:** It's literally a shack on East University Drive, with uneven floors, mismatched tables, and jazz music spilling outside. But they serve seriously good food for breakfast, lunch, and dinner. Try the crawfish omelet for breakfast, a po' boy for lunch, and jambalaya for dinner. They don't serve alcohol but do serve their specialty strawberry lemonade. (*$, (334) 703-0212, creoleandseafoodshack.com*) ❺ **Christopher:** When you want uptown cuisine, instead of down-home eats, drive over to Opelika and have dinner at Christopher. While the building's exterior is pretty plain, you'll find Art Deco silhouettes blended with natural stone and water elements inside, while acid-jazz plays in the background. Foodies will love the menu. Dinner only. (*$–$$, (334) 705-6632*) ❻ **Mike & Ed's Bar-B-Q:** Mike &

Ed's serves the kind of pit-cooked barbecue the South is famous for. With its log-cabin design, campy wall decorations (including a Jim Nabors album stuck to one wall), and large dining area, the vibe is all about good, goofy fun. They have three kinds of sauces, two mustard-based, one tomato-based. (*$, (334) 501-1866*)

Daytime Fun

❶ **Auburn Links at Mill Creek:** It's been voted the "Most Fun Course to Play in the Southeast" and presented with 3 1/2 stars by *Golf Digest*. The Links is a championship course, with a lighted practice range and enough par 5 holes and other features to offer a good challenge. Call for greens fees. (*$–$$, (334) 887-5151, auburnlinks.com*) ❷ **Chewacla State Park:** This 696-acre park has miles of nature trails for hiking and biking, along with rolling hills, streams, lakes, and waterfalls. Fishing, swimming, and boating are options for the outdoors lover at the park's 26-acre lake. You can also wade around and do some boulder-hopping. (*Free, (800) ALA-PARK, outdooralabama.com*) ❸ **Tuskegee Institute National Historic Site:** Visiting here will give you a history lesson you can't get anywhere

else. Start with the **George Washington Carver Museum**, which chronicles his pioneering research that paved the way for alternative fuel development and improved agricultural methods. From there, take the ranger-led tour of **The Oaks**, the stately home built for Tuskegee's first president and founder, Booker T. Washington. Like most of Tuskegee's buil-dings, The Oaks was designed by Institute faculty, then built by faculty and students. It's located on the campus of present-day Tuskegee University. Call to schedule a tour. (*Free, (334) 727-3301, nps.gov/tuin/*)

Nighttime Fun

❶ **Bodega:** Located at Toomer's Corner, you'll find a college crowd listening to eclectic music by regional jam bands and reggae and jazz ensembles that perform regularly. When there's no band, expect classic psychedelic music on the sound system, a la Tangerine Dream. (*$, (334) 887-5990, bodega-auburn.com*) ❷ **Bourbon Street Bar:** This is a huge place and is where Taylor Hicks often played before winning *American Idol*. The cavernous main stage and bar is at street level, between the first and second floors there's a terrace bar with tables overlooking the street, and on top another bar and small outdoor patio. The inside is sort of a French Quarter-meets-roadhouse look. You can find live music here almost every night of the week. (*$, (334) 887-1166, bourbonstreetbar.net*) ❸ **War Eagle Supper Club:** First, you'll need a membership card to get inside. (Don't worry: they're just $2 and anyone can buy one.) Inside this rowdy mainstay of Auburn nightlife you'll find several bars, a main stage (for live music), and a patio out back. You will not, however, find anything resembling supper—War Eagle stopped being an actual supper club years ago. Out on the back deck, check out the Shot Bus, an old, broken down school bus converted into a bar serving only, well, shots. (*$, (334) 821-4455, wareaglesupperclub.com*)

Shopping

❶ **Big Blue Bookstore:** This is Auburn's number one place to buy Tiger gear. While you can actually get textbooks here (not that you'll need them), what most game-day fans buy is stuff from the inventory of just about anything you can think of emblazoned with a Tiger. Salt and pepper shakers in the likeness of Aubie? They're here. You get the idea. (*(334) 821-4440, bigbluebookstore.com*)

❷ **Clothing:** Shoppers looking for a new wardrobe—or part of one—should head down to Toomer's Corner and start strolling along either Magnolia Avenue or College Street. It doesn't matter if you go north or south, east or west; either

way you'll find great shops run by local, independent retailers. Some standouts are **The Buzz, Buckelews**, and the **Back Porch**. ❸ **Easterday Antiques and Fine Art:** Located in Opelika, this place is for the serious antique collector. On a given day, you might see an oaken table dating to the 1600s, Victorian-era estate jewelry, or a desk dating back to the Revolutionary War. But even if you're not a big-time collector, it's worth a visit. Hours vary; call ahead. (*(334) 749-6407, easterdayantiques.com*) ❹ **Rattling Gourd Gallery:** You'll find this off-the-wall gallery in Loachapoka, just down the road. Here you can find unique, handcrafted items by local crafters and artisans, as well as exotic imported items. (*(334) 502-3006, rattlinggourdgallery.com*)

FLORIDA

University of Florida: 49,693 students
Gainesville, FL: pop. 239,114
Ben Hill Griffin Stadium: seats 88,548
Colors: Orange and Blue
Nickname: Gators
Mascot: Albert and Alberta
Phone: (352) 375-4683

RVs can arrive 6 p.m. Friday and park for free at Park & Ride lot next to Hilton Hotel, off 34th Street. RV parking is first-come, first-served. Tailgating starts 6 a.m. game day; doesn't stop until 12 noon Sunday when everybody leaves. Open-container laws strictly enforced.

Shuttle Info: RTS Gator Aider provides shuttle service from multiple off-campus locations, $6 per game, $30 per season. Shuttles run 3 hours before kickoff, until 1 hour after game ends.

Gators Media Partners: 106.3-FM WAFC, 1480-AM WVOI

In 1905 the state of Florida, under the Buckman Act, reorganized its higher education system and combined all of the white men's schools (there were five of them) to create the University of Florida. The new school opened in Gainesville in 1906 with 102 students. (The Buckman Act also designated Florida State University—as a women's school—and the State Normal School for Colored People—now Florida A&M University.)

Well, Florida's grown in the past hundred years. Now Florida is the third largest university in America with about 50,000 students. It also has the eighth-largest budget (almost $2 billion annually) and the second-most National Merit Scholars enrolled (just behind Harvard).

It's a successful school with an equally successful football program. The Gators started to play in 1906 and within a few years began rivalries with some familiar foes including South Carolina, Auburn, Georgia, and Alabama.

The Gators first went to a bowl game in 1952, beating Tulsa in the Gator Bowl. The team's first major bowl game wasn't as successful, a loss to Missouri in the 1965 Sugar Bowl.

But the following year, Heisman Trophy winner Steve Spurrier led the Gators to a 9-2 record and the Orange Bowl, where Florida beat Georgia Tech 27–12. Then the slump began. It lasted nearly two decades. In the mid-1980s the team improved and finished first in the SEC standings in 1984 and 1985, but NCAA probation meant it couldn't claim the conference crown.

But it was in the 1990s that the Gators dominated, led by a coach named Steve Spurrier. Yep, the same guy. He led the Gators to a first-place finish in the conference that year, but the team was still on probation, so it was the next year when Florida came in first and got to claim its first SEC crown.

In Spurrier's 11 years as head coach, the Gators won six SEC championships and, in 1996, its first national championship. He also coached Florida's only other Heisman Trophy winner, Danny Wuerffel (1996). Who says you can't go home again?

The second national championship came as the school celebrated its centennial year of football. It was a convincing victory against a team most felt the Gators didn't deserve to be on the field with.

Throughout the 2006 season, fans and media expected Ohio State to battle USC for the national championship. As the season progressed, OSU didn't disappoint, dominating their opponents and entering the BCS Championship Game undefeated. But USC did disappoint, losing to UCLA in its final regular-season game (their second loss). That opened a door, and Florida snuck in to the big game ranked number two behind Ohio State.

The Buckeyes were supposed to roll, and after returning the opening kickoff for a touchdown, it looked like they would. But second-year coach Urban Meyers's Gators took over and buried the Buckeyes 41–14.

The win also made NCAA history. Florida became the first school to hold the national championship in basketball and football at the same time.

School Mascot

It's not often a fan gets to name a team, and the team doesn't even know it's being named. Believe it or not, that's how the Gators became the Gators.

A 1948 newspaper story explains how Jacksonville lawyer Austin Miller and his father, Phillip, went to a store to order pennants and banners for the University of Florida in 1907, a year after the football team first took the field. After looking at samples with the Yale bulldog and the Princeton tiger on them, and then making their banner selections, the store manager asked for Florida's logo to put on the banners. That's when the Millers realized Florida didn't have one.

So Austin Miller suggested Alligators, since they are native to Florida. The store manager said no other school was using that name, so that's what they put on the banners. It turned out to be a popular name with students, and it stuck.

The costumed Gators you see roaming The Swamp on game day aren't exactly the ones the Millers envisioned, but Albert made his first appearance in the 1960s, and Alberta came along in 1986.

Game-Day Traditions

Gator Jaws

There's the Gator Walk, but it's the Gator Jaws that the nation immediately identifies with Florida. The taunt was created about 20 years ago by the Pride of the Sunshine Marching Band. Off-and-on throughout the game, the band plays the theme to the movie *Jaws*, and Gator fans use their outstretched arms to simulate a gator's mouth "chomping" to the beat, ostensibly devouring their opponent.

Gator Growl

Today this 80-plus-year tradition is the self-proclaimed largest student-run pep rally in the world (there's a volunteer staff of 500), as students, alumni, and fans come together for a night of festivities to prepare for the game. You need to bring your Gator spirit, but at least you don't have to bring your weight in wood anymore.

You used to, though—if you were a freshman.

The Gator Growl began in 1924 as a descendent of part of Florida's home-

GATORADE

The drink of athletes, and the field shower of winning coaches, was created by several doctors at the University of Florida in 1965 for the football team. They formulated it to aid players and keep them hydrated . . . hence the name. It seemed to work.

The team first used it officially in 1967, and that year they beat Georgia Tech to win their first Orange Bowl title. The Georgia Tech coach, when asked why his team lost, is reported to have answered: "We didn't have Gatorade. That made the difference."

Two years later the Kansas City Chiefs officially used the drink and went on to win the Super Bowl. They said the drink helped them win the ring.

One of the doctors, Dr. Robert Cade, had patented the brew and in 1973 sold it to Stokely-Van Camp to produce. Since then it's been sold a couple more times (PepsiCo owns it now) and has become a money-making cultural icon.

Florida Fight Song

"The Orange and Blue"

On, brave old Flor-i-da, just keep on marching on your way!

On, brave old Flor-i-da, and we will cheer you on your play! Rah! Rah! Rah!

And as you march a-long, we'll sing our victory song anew

With all your might Go on and Fight Gators

Fight for Dixie's rightly proud of you

Chorus:

So give a cheer for the Orange and Blue,

Waving for-ev-er, forever

Pride of old Flor-i-da, May she droop nev-er

We'll sing a song for the flag to-day, Cheer for the team at play!

On to the goal we'll fight our way for Flor-i-da.

coming festivities called Dad's Day. There was a large bonfire between the school's two dorms (there were just two then), and freshmen had to bring their weight in wood to burn and "fire-up" enthusiasm for the next day's game. There was also a dance and boxing matches.

Today the Gator Growl is a festival with live performances, pyrotechnics and light shows, music, comedy, and has featured headliners such as Bob Hope, George Burns, Robin Williams, and Bill Cosby. (To learn more log on to gatorgrowl.org.)

Visiting Florida

Best known, of course, as home to the university, Gainesville is also popular with outdoor enthusiasts and was once named *Money Magazine*'s most livable city in America. With several parks, waterways, and trails nearby, there's always something to keep you busy when not watching the Gators. Of course, there's stuff to do inside, too.

Where to Stay

❶ **Herlong Mansion:** On the outside it's a very large, Greek-revival mansion, straight out of a movie. Inside the B&B you'll be walking on mahogany-inlaid floors and staring at 10 fireplaces, leaded glass windows, and other

architectural details. There are six rooms, three suites, and four adjacent cottages. Weekend rates run $99–$159 for a room, $179–$189 for suites. Cottages are $159–$269. Tack on another $20 if you're staying during a special event weekend. (*(352) 466-3322, herlong.com*) ❷ **Laurel Oak Inn:** This B&B offers five guest rooms, each with a gas fireplace or wood stove. The rooms are all furnished with period antiques, ceiling fans, and high-end linens, plus bath accessories. Rooms run $115–$150. (*(352) 373-4535, laureloakinn.com*)

❸ **Lochloosa Harbor RV Park:** Located on the shores of Lochloosa Lake, there are 35 full hookup RV sites, plus six cottages with kitchenettes. The lake is full of fish,

ALMA MATER

"UF Alma Mater"

Florida, our Alma Mater
Thy glorious name we praise
All thy loyal sons and daughters
A joyous song shall raise
Where a palm and pine are blowing
Where southern seas are flowing
Shine forth thy noble Gothic walls
Thy lovely vineclad halls
'Neath the Orange and Blue
victorious our love shall never fail
There's no other name so glorious
All hail, Florida, hail.

and the park has a bait shop with everything you'll need. You'll get a chance to see eagles, osprey, and blue and white heron as well. You won't get a chance to see cable TV or the Internet, though. Sites are $22. (*(352) 481-2114, lochloosaharbor.com*) ❹ **Magnolia Plantation:** This B&B has so many rooms it's really almost a small hotel. There are five guestrooms in the main house, a French Second Empire Victorian mansion. But Magnolia's also has six separate cottages, bringing the number of guestrooms to 18. Wine and snacks are served every evening. Rooms go for $99–$150 in the main house and $195–$330 in the cottages. (*(352) 375-6653, magnoliabnb.com*) **❺ Reitz Union Hotel:** The hotel is perfectly located for game day, offering on-campus accommodations. There are 36 rooms, ranging from basic rooms with two double beds to the much fancier Executive Suite. Normally, a standard room is $79 for a single person, while the Executive Suite is $114 for two people. Oh, but not during football season. Hope you're feeling lucky: during home-game weekends, getting a room requires winning the lottery—literally. Room lottery applications must be postmarked by April 1st, and lottery results are sent out by May 15th. (*(352) 392-2151, union.ufl.edu/hotel/*) **❻ Travelers Campground:** In neighboring Alachua, this RV park provides 42 full hookup sites in their overnight section. The campground has a pool, picnic tables, and a recreation hall. Some sites can be a little hard to get in and out of. The rate is $20. (*(386) 462-2505, travelerscampground.com*)

Where to Eat

TAILGATE SUPPLIES: **❶ Ward's Supermarket:** This locally owned grocery store is a favorite with Gainesville residents. Ward's makes a habit of using local growers to supply their fruits and veggies, even their honey. You'll often find juices and dairy products not stocked at larger, regional stores and fresh spices for half the price you'd pay for prepackaged spices at larger supermarkets. (*(352) 372-1741*)

SPORTS BARS: **❷ Gator City Sports Grill:** It used to

be the Purple Porpoise Oyster Bar, a beloved Gainesville watering hole. But times change, and now it's Gator City. It still has all the features that made the Porpoise great, including a front and back room, each with a bar. In the front, there are big-screen TVs broadcasting the game. In the back, you'll find pool tables and video games. (*$, (352) 377-7333*) ❸ **Gator's Dockside:** Part of a chain of bars in Florida, Gator's provides an abundance of TVs, complete with huge big-screens, for watching the game of your choice. They also seat people according to the team they are here to see. Relax Gator fans, they won't seat any Vols next to you. They're also family-friendly, so bringing kids isn't a problem. This is a very popular place, so expect big crowds and some parking challenges. (*$, (352) 338-4445, gatorsdockside.com*) ❹ **The Swamp:** No, not the stadium, the former professor's home. Now it's a two-story gathering place that's both a restaurant and bar. Patrons love the outdoor dining, and on game days the management hauls a big-screen TV outside. The menu of soups, salads, sandwiches and wraps, and grilled entrées is pretty good, too. (*$, (352) 377-9267, swamprestaurant.com*)

RESTAURANTS: ❺ **Emiliano's Café:** Another local favorite in a town full of good restaurants. The menu is pan-Latin—dishes show influences from places like Puerto Rico, Spain, Cuba, and South America. The atmosphere pays homage to the café's Latin heritage with walls painted in rich colors, jazz music in the background, and colorful, bold artwork on the walls. (*$–$$, (352) 375-7381, emilianoscafe.com*) ❻ **Paramount Grill:** According to locals, this tiny restaurant (it seats 32 people) is one of the best in the region. The chef/owner uses fresh local Florida produce, meats, and seafood to create new-American cuisine. If you're on a budget, try Paramount for lunch, but dinner gives you the whole effect. The interior is a long, narrow space with pale wood floors and sepia photos from previous generations of the owner's family. (*$–$$, (352) 378-3398*) ❼ **South Beach Diner:** Here's where to go for breakfast. Or lunch. Or dinner. Or a late-night bite. It's open around the clock. The menu includes beignets, four tasty omelet choices, a variety of "egg and" combos (bacon, ham, prime rib, fish), pancakes, and a prime rib hash. Yes, prime rib hash. The diner's housed in what used to be a Burger King, but don't let that scare you away. (*$, (352) 372-6244*)

Daytime Fun

❶ **Biking:** Gainesville has 77 miles of bike lanes and trails, more than any other town in Florida. The 16-mile-long **Gainesville-Hawthorne State Trail** is paved and offers an easy, relaxing ride through parts of **Paynes Prairie State Preserve** and **Lochloosa Wildlife Area**. (*Free, (352) 466-3397, floridastateparks.org*) A more challenging experience lies up the road at **Alachua's San Felasco Hammock Preserve State Park**. San Felasco's trails are designed for mountain bikers and range from beginner to advanced. (*$, (386) 462-7905, floridastateparks.org*) If you need a bike, you can rent one from **Recycled Bikes** (*(352) 372-4890*) or **Bikes & More** (*(352) 373-6574*). ❷ **Devil's Millhopper State Geological Site:** This is a huge sinkhole containing an actual rain forest. Really. It was formed centuries ago, when the roof of an underground limestone cavern collapsed, leaving a giant bowl-shaped crater. Thanks to 12 springs trickling down its walls, and a much cooler environment, lush vegetation runs riot with species you'll see nowhere else in Florida. (*$, (352) 955-2008,*

floridastateparks.org) ❸ **Florida Museum of Natural History:** Fun for the family, the museum just added a cool butterfly rainforest—a four-story, outdoor enclosure with waterfalls, a walking trail, lush plant life, and hordes of live butterflies. You can also see fossil bones dating back to when Florida was part of the ocean floor, giant shark jaws, and a 15-foot-tall ground sloth. Located on campus. (*$, (352) 846-2000, flmnh.ufl.edu*) ❹ **Gainesville Rock Gym:** The gym offers an affordable climbing adventure for climbers of all ages and skill levels. All you need is a partner, some comfortable sportswear, and sneakers. A day pass, gear rental, and free belay class will run $18 for adults, $14 for kids 12 or younger. (*$$, (352) 335-4789 x 5, gainesvillerock.com*)

Nighttime Fun

❶ **:08 Seconds:** Boot, scoot, and boogie in this hip country bar, with two-stepping, line dancing, and free dance lessons for anyone who's feeling left-footed. If you're not up for the dance floor, you've got drink specials and pool tables to keep you occupied. Oh, about the :08 . . . it's a rodeo thing. (*$, (352) 384-0888, 8-seconds.com*) ❷ **Eddie C's:** It's casual, a little scruffy, and plays more live music than any other club in Gainesville. Some of the bands are darned good, and others are, well, not as good. But you get live music almost every night. In between band sets, you can shoot some pool, throw darts, or play video games. (*$, (352) 378-9185, eddiecs.com*) ❸ **Hippodrome State Theatre:** If you want to skip the college scene, try live theater inside Gainesville's former Federal Building and Post Office. It's a grand looking structure with a main stage; a cinema showing foreign, limited-release, and avant-garde films; and an art gallery. The theatre, one of the nation's leading regional playhouses, produces a mix of traditional and modern plays, with the odd musicals thrown in. (*$$$, (352) 375-4477, thehipp.org*) ❹ **XS:** You want to dance? Here's where you can dance into the wee hours, right next door to Gator City Sports Grill (see #2 in Where to Eat). Along with a large stage and dance floor, XS has a sofa-filled lounge where the young and the restless can catch their breath between dances. Most nights feature '80s sounds for dancers. (*$, (352) 377-7333*)

Shopping

❶ **The Gator Shop:** Located on West University Avenue, just north of the stadium, this has been the place to get your Gator gear since 1946. The Gator Shop stocks everything a Florida fan could wish for—clothing, collectibles, autographed merchandise, automotive items, even fishing lures. *((352) 376-5191, gatorshop.com)* ❷ **Thornebrook Gallery:** This gallery offers works of regional and internationally known artists. Its interior is full of hand-blown iridescent bowls, unique pieces of jewelry, pottery, and other objets d'art. Check out their collection of handmade kaleidoscopes. *((800) 449-4947, thornebrookgallery.com)* ❸ **Thornebrook Village:** Quite a few of Gainesville's unique, independent stores can be found here, including **Thornebrook Gallery**. This worthwhile shopping destination is built to resemble a flower-filled tropical resort with open-air, covered breezeways connecting buildings around a central plaza. You can amble into everything from a chocolatier to a day spa to clothing boutiques, a bead store, antique stores, and more. *(thornebrookvillage.com)*

GEORGIA

University of Georgia: 33,405 students
Athens, GA: pop. 100,266
Sanford Stadium: seats 92,746
Colors: Red and Black
Nickname: Bulldogs
Mascot: Uga (live), Hairy Dawg (costumed)
Phone: (706) 542-7275, (706) 357-9613 Prestige Parking

RVs arrive 6 p.m. Friday; park at Prestige Parking three blocks away from stadium. RV parking is $75 a weekend. Tailgating starts as early as 7 a.m. game day and ends 2 hours after game. Alcohol is limited to North Campus Quad and D. W. Brooks Mall. Tailgaters must provide own power source. Alcohol-free, family-friendly areas available in North and South campus.

Shuttle Info: All parking within easy walking distance. No shuttles needed.

Bulldogs Media Partner: 750-AM WSB

When Georgia's governor needed someone to build his state's educational system and open the state's university, he turned to a Yale man—but not just any Yale man. Abraham Baldwin may have been a Connecticut native, but he was Georgia's representative to the Continental Congress and, later, represented the Peach State in the U.S. House of Representatives and the Senate.

The University of Georgia was the first state-chartered university in America, and Baldwin was the school's first president. He left the school when it opened for classes in 1801, having accomplished what he was hired to do.

Like many southern schools, Georgia closed its doors in 1863 as students and faculty left to fight in the Civil War. It reopened in 1866.

About 15 years later a different type of founding father came to the Athens campus. Dr. Charles Herty was hired to teach chemistry, but he also taught football. He introduced the sport to students, formed the first team, and laid out the first field. This founding father of Georgia football then led his team to its first game in January 1892 against Mercer College.

The next month he and a former classmate from Johns Hopkins University—who taught at Auburn—arranged for a game between the two schools. Auburn may have won, but it was the start of the oldest football rivalry in the South.

In the century since, Georgia has built one of the nation's top football programs. The Bulldogs were coached by Glenn "Pop" Warner in the mid-1890s, but it was Vince Dooley who was the team's most successful coach, compiling a record from 1964–1988 of 201-77-10, 6 SEC titles, and the 1980 national championship.

Georgia boasts two Heisman Trophy winners: Frank Sinkwich in 1942 and Herschel Walker in 1982. It also is the only program to have three different players to be named Super Bowl MVP: Jake Scott (Miami Dolphins), Terrell Davis (Denver Broncos), and Hines Ward (Pittsburgh Steelers).

School Mascot

I mentioned earlier how it was a Yale man who organized the University of Georgia. Yale's mascot is the bulldog. Georgia's mascot is the bulldog. Coincidence? Probably.

While there are many who claim that's why Georgia is the Bulldogs, the written record most often cited for the nickname doesn't mention that at all. In fact, it was 119 years later, in 1920, when Morgan Blake of the *Atlanta*

Journal wrote, "The Georgia Bulldogs would sound good because there is a certain dignity about a bulldog, as well as ferocity." Another of the paper's writers later that year used the nickname five times in his story about a game against Virginia. That's most likely where the name came from.

The school's live mascot, Uga (named for the school's abbreviation), first graced the sideline in 1956. The pure white English bulldog has become one of the most recognizable mascots in college sports. Uga V was on the cover of *Sports Illustrated* and in the movie *Midnight in the Garden of Good and Evil.*

THE GEORGIA "G"

Georgia's helmet looks a lot like the one the NFL's Green Bay Packers wear. They're just different colors. So who copied whom? Well, no one, really.

In 1964, new Georgia football coach Vince Dooley redesigned the Bulldogs' uniforms, using a red helmet that featured a black "G" on a white background. Former Bulldog John Donaldson's wife designed the logo, and Dooley approved it.

The Georgia "G" was a different design and color than the Green Bay "G" at the time, but Coach Dooley thought it would be best to get the OK from Green Bay to use it. The Packers didn't mind, so that fall the Bulldogs took to the field with the now familiar logo on their helmets.

Since then the Packers' "G" has been tweaked and redesigned so it now looks more like the Georgia "G."

Uga VI represents the school now and is the largest of the line of mascots, weighing in at 55 pounds. (All of Georgia's Ugas have come from the same line owned by the Frank W. "Sonny" Seiler family of Savannah.) On the field Uga has a permanent, air-conditioned, doghouse next to the cheerleaders. Lucky dog.

Not as lucky is the guy (or gal) inside Hairy Dawg, the costumed bulldog mascot prowling the sidelines. It gets hot in Georgia. It gets hotter in that costume.

"Glory, Glory"

(Played after a score)

Glory, glory to old Georgia!
Glory, glory to old Georgia!
Glory, glory to old Georgia!
G-E-O-R-G-I-A.
Glory, glory to old Georgia!
Glory, glory to old Georgia!
Glory, glory to old Georgia!
G-E-O-R-G-I-A.

"Hail Georgia"

(Played after the PAT)

Hail to Georgia down in Dixie!
Our college honored fair and true,
The Red and Black is her standard,
Proudly it waves!
Streaming today and the ages through,
She's the fairest of the Southland,
We'll pledge our love to her for aye,
To that college dear we'll ring a cheer,
All hail to dear old UGA!

Game-Day Traditions
"Between the Hedges"

When Sanford Stadium was dedicated in 1929, the field was surrounded by 1-foot-high English privet hedges that were protected by a fence. It made for a unique playing field. Those hedges became fodder for an Atlanta sportswriter—some say it was the legendary Grantland Rice—who wrote "that the Bulldogs will have their opponent 'between the hedges.'"

The hedges are bigger now, as is the legend, but Bulldog fans are fiercely proud of the tradition and of what their team tends to do to opponents "Between the Hedges" on Saturdays. Of course, the hedges are also material for sports writers in other cities whose teams defeat Georgia in Athens. As one Nashville paper's headline said after Vanderbilt's 2006 upset of the Bulldogs: "Georgia's Hedges Trimmed."

The Chapel Bell

The Chapel was built in 1832, but the ringing of its bell after Georgia victories began in the 1890s. The football field was next to the Chapel then, and after the final whistle, freshman students were forced to run to the Chapel and ring the bell until midnight to celebrate the win.

Today it takes longer to get from the stadium to the Chapel, and freshmen aren't compelled to ring it, but students, alumni, and fans still head to the historic building to ring the bell after a Bulldog win.

Visiting Georgia

Athens has always been a college town. It was named in honor of the center of higher learning in classical Greece. Today it is a lively town with an active music scene that has introduced us to the likes of R.E.M., the B-52's, and Widespread Panic. It is also home to a number of great restaurants and galleries.

Where to Stay

❶ **Country Boy's RV Park:** About 17 miles north of Athens, near Commerce, Country Boy's has 75 pull-through and big-rig accessible sites available with full hookups and basic amenities. The park sometimes has a number of long-term residents here, so call to confirm available space. Sites cost $20. (*(706) 335-5535*)

ALMA MATER

From the hills of Georgia's northland
Beams thy noble brow,
And the sons of Georgia rising
Pledge with sacred vow.

'Neath the pine tree's stately shadow
Spread thy riches rare,
And thy sons, dear Alma Mater,
Will thy treasure share.

And thy daughters proudly join thee,
Take their rightful place,
Side by side into the future,
Equal dreams embrace.

Through the ages, Alma Mater,
Men will look to thee;
Thou the fairest of the Southland
Georgia's Varsity.

Chorus:
Alma Mater, thee we'll honor,
True and loyal be,
Ever crowned with praise and glory,
Georgia, hail to thee.

❷ **Foundry Park Inn & Spa:** This place is a lot of things—a 119-room boutique inn, a conference center, a day spa, a restaurant, a performance space, and a pub. It's also a mix of restored buildings from the 1800s and modern construction. Thanks to some thoughtful planning, the facility succeeds in fusing all these things together into a smoothly functioning whole. Rooms average $125. (*(866) 928-4367, foundryparkinn.com*)

❸ **Grand Oaks Manor:** This B&B started out as the Gum Springs Inn in 1820, serving travelers on the 1805 Federal Road. The inn was rebuilt in 1947, with the original building as a substructure, then renovated as a B&B in 1994. Today, the Colonial Revival-style house offers five guestrooms and three open suites, each with a private bath. Located on 34 partially wooded acres with plenty of deer sightings. No children or pets are allowed. Rooms run $109–159. (*(706) 353-2200, grandoaksmanor.com*)

❹ **Magnolia Terrace Bed & Breakfast:** Located a few steps from UGA's Old North Campus and built in 1902, this B&B looks like the kind of happy, Victorian-style house you'd find in a Frank Capra movie. Inside, you'll find eight guestrooms furnished with antiques and large, private baths. Many rooms also have working fireplaces. Complimentary port, sherry, or single malt scotch is available every evening.

Room rates are $85–$150. (*(706) 548-3860, bbonline.com/ga/magnoliaterrace*)

❺ Pine Lake Campground: A small RV park with 36 sites, this campground is nestled around two peaceful lakes near Bishop, about 12 miles south of UGA. All sites have full hookups, and there are some pleasant nature trails, a playground, and basic restroom and shower facilities. The lakes are stocked with farm-raised catfish, bass, and bluegill (a campground permit is required to fish; catches are paid for by the pound). Sites run $23–$24. (*(706) 769-5486*) **❻ The Pottery Campground:** Near Commerce, this RV campground has 51 sites, but they're large and well paved. Each site also has a fireplace/grill, concrete picnic table, and light post with a graduated on/off switch. Full hookups are available. Sites will set you back $20. (*(800) 223-0667, cravenpottery.com*)

Where to Eat

TAILGATE SUPPLIES: **❶ Daily Groceries Co-op:** This funky little organic food and health store sells organic local produce, groceries, supplements, and other good-for-you things. Daily Groceries can also supply you with ready-made dips, salads, and sandwiches. While the store is a true co-op, it's also open to the

public. But if you want to join, "investing" members get a 5 percent discount with an annual $50 fee. (*(706) 548-1732, dailygroceries.org*)

SPORTS BARS: ❷ **The Arch Bar:** Owned and operated by UGA alumni, the large, brick-walled space has cozy leather furniture, high ceilings, and nice touches like stained-glass windows. Here you can watch football on the flat-screen TV, while sipping a top-shelf martini or margarita, or just stick to the Arch's selection of microbrew beers. (*$, (706) 548-0300, thearchbar.com*)
❸ **Broad Street Bar & Grill:** The walls here are crammed with UGA Dawg memorabilia from floor to ceiling, which may be part of the reason this bar is such a popular hangout before and after games. Other reasons probably include the extensive menu (including prime rib), their beers on tap (ranging from exotics like Hoegaarden to tried-and-true domestics), or signature cocktails and 101 different house shots. (*$, (706) 548-5187*) ❹ **Eastwood Pub:** Eastwood has a good selection of pub-style beers, plus half a dozen TVs tuned to your favorite game. One TV is located out on the porch. When it's not game day, the pub has a full lineup of live music and other diversions. (*$, (706) 549-7711,*

eastwoodpub.com) ❺ **Nowhere Bar:** This is the place to go if you can't get a ticket to the game. Owned by a former UGA linebacker, the place rocks on game days, as fans live and breathe every second of the game. More than 100 beers on tap keep the place full of happy patrons playing darts, pool, Golden Tee, or video games. There's also live music from time to time. (*$, (706) 546-4742*)

RESTAURANTS: ❻ **The Basil Press:** Dishes like Prince Edward mussels or oysters on the half shell and paella with duck, andouille sausage, and shellfish on saffron rice and vegetables let you know you've gone upscale. Open for lunch and dinner, with brunch on Sundays. (*$–$$, (706) 227-8926, acoyaas. com/bp/bphome.htm*) ❼ **Clocked!:** This is the kind of zany, hip, just-crazy-enough-to-work joint that could only exist in an equally hip, zany town like Athens. The décor is funky and groovy, and so is the menu. They serve hamburgers as big as your head (I'm presuming your head isn't *that* big) topped with everything from fried eggs to peanut butter (though not on the same burger). There's also a brown-butter hazelnut pasta. (*$, (706) 548-9175, clocked.us*) ❽ **Harry Bissett's New Orleans Café & Oyster Bar:** One of

Athens's favorite restaurants, popular with both students and adults and located across from Georgia's North Campus, the building still sports tin ceilings and brickwork from its days as a bank in the 1860s. While the New Orleans-influenced menu drips with tasty dishes, barbecued shrimp is a favorite among regulars. Harry's serves lunch and dinner, with brunch on Saturdays and Sundays. ($–$$, (706) 353-7065, harry bissetts.net)

➒ **Peaches Fine Foods**: For lunch—and only lunch—in classic, Southern, meat-n-three style, head over to Peaches for some of the best down-home cooking you've ever tasted. It's all served cafeteria style (another meat-n-three tradition), so you can eyeball the food before you choose it. The menu changes every day, as well. ($, (706) 613-5334, peachesfinefoods.com)

Daytime Fun

➊ **Double-Barreled Cannon**: Built at a local foundry in 1863, the idea was to arm it with two cannonballs connected by several feet of chain. When fired, the balls and chain would fly out, spinning bola-style, to cut down anything in its path. During its only test-firing it worked a little too well—the projectile plowed up an acre of ground, tore up a cornfield, and mowed down saplings. When the chain broke apart, the balls flew in opposite directions, one killing a cow in a distant field and the other knocking the chimney off a log cabin. Not surprisingly, it's the only one of its kind. You'll find it on the City Hall lawn at College and

Hancock avenues, pointing north. ❷ **T. R. R. Cobb House:** This 1830s house with its unusual octagonal wings has traveled 70 miles from Stone Mountain, Georgia, to Athens. The house was originally the home of T. R. R. Cobb, an Athens lawyer, Confederate legislator, and soldier. Cobb died during the war, and the house went through a succession of owners, serving as everything from a church to a frat house. For 20 years it sat moldering on cinderblocks outside Atlanta. Now the house is back. It's taken 2 years to fully restore and is now a Civil War–era museum. (*$, (706) 369-3513, trrcobbhouse.org*) ❸ **The Tree That Owns Itself:** I know, it doesn't make sense at first, so follow along. The tree, located on the corner of Dearing and Finley Streets, is the beneficiary of Colonel William Jackson, who owned the land where the tree stood. Jackson loved that tree, a large white oak, and the shade it provided. He loved it enough to deed his tree 8 feet of land surrounding its trunk on all sides, as well as ownership of itself. The tree stood, proudly self-owned, until 1942, when it succumbed to heart-rot and windstorms. Four years later, the local garden club planted a sapling grown from one of

the tree's acorns (a botanical heir) right in the same spot. Locals call the oak the world's most unusual heir and property owner. And it's never paid a cent in property taxes, either. ❹ **Sandy Creek Nature Center and Sandy Creek Park:** Both offer lots of ways to enjoy the great outdoors. The Nature Center has plenty of hiking trails winding through its 200 acres of woodland and marshland, which include a live animal

exhibit. (*Free, (706) 613-3615, sandycreeknaturecenter.com*) The park offers lots of family-oriented options, with a beach, fishing, children's playgrounds, softball, volleyball, and shelters for picnics. You can rent paddleboats and canoes, too. (*Free–$, (706) 613-3631, sandycreekpark.com*) ❺ **UGA Golf Course:** This Robert Trent Jones–designed course is a public course, but that doesn't make it easy. The course's layout is pretty demanding, from the hilly terrain to the typical Jones strategic design. UGA just renovated the entire course, leveling fairways, improving its greens, and adding tee boxes. (*$$–$$$, (800) 9-DOG-TEE, golfcourse.uga.edu*)

Nighttime Fun

❶ **40 Watt Club:** This is the place that gave us the B-52's and R.E.M. You can still hear up-and-coming local bands, some just starting out, while others come with a loyal following. The club also books national bands, and just to mix it up a little, 40 Watt also hosts a late-night disco party. The club has two bars. While you'll need cash for admission, you can use your credit card at the bar. (*$–$$, (706) 549-7871, 40watt.com*) ❷ **Barcode:** This place looks more like it belongs in Europe than the South. It's dark and cavernous, sparse and cool, but the club draws them in to drink, play pool or darts, and dance. (*$, (706) 613-5557*)

❸ **Georgia Theater:** This is a popular stop for your Athens music tour. Once a movie theater, it gives local college rock bands (along with some blues and Southern rock) a place to jam long past midnight. They also run a late-night disco several times a week. Last year the theatre renovated its stage design and sound system. (*$–$$, (706) 549-9918, georgiatheatre.com*) ❹ **Last Call:** A popular place to see decent regional cover and "tribute" bands, as well as some national acts. While their hippie/jam scene has faded a bit, the growing popularity of several local country-rock acts resulted in this vast bar's Friday nights being reserved for that genre. (*$, (706) 353-8869, athenslastcall.com*)

Shopping

❶ **Clayton Street:** This is the road traveled for several original, unique stores in Athens. Among the highlights are **Wuxtry Records'** vast collection of

mainstream and obscure vinyl, CDs, cassettes, publications, and other knickknacks; **Helix** and its novelty items like chopsticks, Elvis magnets, and butterfly mobiles, as well as its handmade pottery and jewelry; **Frontier's** handmade beeswax candles and candle holders, carved or decorated with pressed dried flowers; and **Heery's Clothes Closet's** preppy but funky outfits with brands like MaxStudio, Laundry, Lilly Pulitzer, Cole Hann, and Franco Sarto. ❷ **The Red Zone:** Located on Clayton Street, this store is

UGA's largest retailer of officially licensed Bulldog clothing and memorabilia. Here, you can pick up sweatpants, sweatshirts, jewelry, billiard balls, office supplies, flags, toys, and anything else capable of being decorated with a UGA logo. The store makes no bones about it: they welcome dogs of all shapes and sizes, but won't allow Yellow Jackets, Gators, Tigers, Tar Heels, Vols, beggars, thieves, or panhandlers on the premises. (*(706) 353-8500, ugaredzone.com*)

KENTUCKY

University of Kentucky: 25,397 students
Lexington, KY: pop. 268,080
Commonwealth Stadium: seats 67,606
Colors: Blue and White
Nickname: Wildcats
Mascot: Scratch and Wildcat (costumed);
　Blue (live)
Phone: (800) 928-CATS

RVs start arriving Friday at 6 p.m., park for free on Press Avenue. Early RV arrivals wait in holding area at the Soccer/Softball lot. Parking attendant will issue early RVs a number upon arrival. RVs then released into Press Avenue lot in numerical order when area opens. Any campus parking lot designated "E" is available after 3:30 p.m. on Friday (unless otherwise posted) and all day Saturday and Sunday. A non-reserved disabled lot is located at the corner of University Drive and Farm Road—free shuttles provided. Tailgating starts 8 a.m. game day, ends at day's end. Golf carts allowed in RV lots only. No open alcoholic containers at stadium. The following items require prior approval: oversized grills, banners/signage recognizing businesses, generators, and tents over 10 x 10 square feet.

Shuttle Info: Free shuttle service available from Press Avenue and Tobacco Research Building to Stadium.

Wildcats Media Partners: 630-AM WLAP-AM, 98.1-FM WBUL

John Bowman wanted a university in Lexington. So, he sought and gained funding and pushed his dream through politics and construction to open Agricultural and Mechanical College in 1865. Known as A&M College, the school was a publicly chartered department of Kentucky University. In 1878 A&M separated from Kentucky University (now known as Transylvania University, which has nothing to do with vampires). A&M's

name was changed to State University in 1908 and then to the University of Kentucky in 1916.

Football at A&M College had a dubious inauguration. The first game was in 1881 against its old partner, Kentucky University. A&M won 7 1/4–1. Really. No one knows how they scored that game, but it resembled rugby more than football. That first season A&M went 2-1, and then they pulled the plug. The school didn't play football for the next nine seasons.

But the game came back, of course, and as the University of Kentucky, the school has had a rich football history.

Perhaps the best team UK ever put on the field—at the very least of the era—was the 1898 team known to fans as "The Immortals." The Immortals are the only undefeated, untied, and un-scored upon team in UK football history, going 7-0-0 that year with a combined score of 180-0. The other amazing feat of The Immortals was that the average weight per player of that team was just 147 pounds.

Kentucky was the first SEC school to introduce football, the first SEC school to have a player win the Outland Trophy (Bob Gain in 1950), and the first SEC school to sign, and play, an African American player (Nat Northington in 1967). It was also the first SEC home to a coach named Paul "Bear" Bryant, who took the Wildcats to their first bowl game (the one and only Great Lakes Bowl in 1947) and is still the most successful coach in UK history.

It was Bryant who coached what is commonly thought of as the biggest win in Kentucky football history: a 13–7 upset of Oklahoma in the 1951 Sugar Bowl. The win broke OU's 31-game winning streak, which is the seventh longest in college football history.

Some great players have worn the blue and white, too, including George Blanda, Howard Schnellenberger, and Art Still.

School Mascot

Kentucky got its nickname the way a lot of schools did in the early 1900s—from a simile someone made about the way the team played in a game. In this case the game was a win against Illinois in 1909. Commandant Carbusier, who was the head of the military department at what was then commonly called State College, said the football team "fought like Wildcats." Students and alumni liked the association, so they kept it.

There is a live Wildcat mascot, Blue, who lives full-time at the Kentucky Department of Fish and Wildlife's Salato Wildlife Center. You can visit him there, if you'd like. Blue is the most recent live mascot; others before him have had names such as Tom (the first mascot in 1921), TNT, Whiskers, Colonel, and Hot Tamale. I'm not sure how that last one was named.

Kentucky Fight Song

"On, On, U of K"

On, on, U of K, we are right for the
fight today,

Hold that ball and hit that line;

Ev'ry Wildcat star will shine;

We'll fight, fight, fight, for the blue
and white

As we roll to that goal, Varsity,

And we'll kick, pass and run, 'till the
battle is won,

And we'll bring home the victory.

The mascots you'll see stalking the field on game day are of the costumed variety and named Wildcat ("born" in 1976) and Scratch (who debuted in 1996).

Game-Day Traditions
Catwalk

Football often takes a backseat to basketball at Kentucky (that was one reason why "Bear" Bryant left the school), and many fans say that's one reason why the Catwalk disappeared as a pregame Wildcats ritual sometime in the 1980s. But a couple of years ago fans decided to bring the Catwalk back—led by Coach Rick Brooks's daughter, Kerri.

Like team walks at other schools, the Catwalk allows fans to encourage the team as players make their way to the field. At UK the Catwalk begins at the Nutter

Field House and extends to Commonwealth Stadium. Fans line up a couple of hours before kickoff to cheer the 'Cats into battle.

"My Old Kentucky Home"

Every game day the Kentucky Band plays, and the crowd sings, "My Old Kentucky Home." Written by Stephen Foster in 1853 and adopted as the state song in 1928, the song was inspired by a visit to his cousins' home, Federal Hill Mansion, which appears on the back of the Kentucky state quarter. Although some of the words have been changed to be less offensive to African Americans, the original lyrics describe life on a slave plantation; the abolitionist Frederick Douglass found the song sympathetic to slaves.

In addition to being a UK tradition, the song is also sung each year at the Kentucky Derby, although accompanied by that other Kentucky school's band.

ALMA MATER

Hail Kentucky, Alma Mater!
Loyal sons and daughters sing;
Sound her praise with voice united;
To the breeze her colors fling.
To the blue and white be true;
Badge triumphant age on age;
Blue, the sky that o'er us bends;
White, Kentucky's stainless page.

"My Old Kentucky Home"

The sun shines bright on my old Kentucky home,
'Tis summer, the people are gay;
The corntop's ripe and the meadows in the bloom,
While the birds make music all the day.
The young folks roll on the little cabin floor,
All merry, all happy, and bright;
By-n-by hard times come a-knocking at the door,
Then, my old Kentucky home, good-night!
Weep no more, my lady,
Oh! Weep no more, today!
We will sing one song for my old Kentucky home,
For my old Kentucky home far away.

Visiting Kentucky

This town loves the University of Kentucky. Heck, its area code (859) spells UKY. But this town, and state, loves the horses, too. Lexington is home to the Kentucky Horse Park, Keeneland, and the Red Mile tracks. And, if you're in need of some Lexington trivia to impress people, the Jif plant here makes more peanut butter than any other factory in the world.

Where to Stay

❶ Bed & Breakfast at Silver Springs: It's only 5 miles from downtown Lexington, but you'll feel like you're far away on vacation. The house is surrounded by 21 acres, complete with horses, a barn, and a springhouse. There are three guest rooms, one with a private bath; the other two share a bath. There's also a two-bedroom cottage full of antiques and collectibles, equipped with a full kitchen. Room rates vary by length of stay and area events, but typically, rooms run $139–$199. The cottage will set you back $249–$299 and may require a two-night minimum stay. ((877) 255-1784, bbsilver

springsfarm.com) ❷ **George Clarke House:** Located in the town's historic district, this B&B offers four very plush guestrooms with private baths. The house is beautifully decorated and maintained in high 1890s Victorian style, with an attention to detail that's almost uncanny. Even the proprietress is in period dress. Rooms run $249–$315 during football weekends. (*(866) 436-1890, georgeclarkehouse.com*) ❸ **Gratz Park Inn:** Originally the first medical clinic west of the Allegheny Mountains, this historic brick property now offers 44 rooms, including 6 suites. The inn is within walking distance to the University of Kentucky and a host of other downtown attractions. The on-site restaurant is one of Lexington's best. During football season, rooms run $149–$185, while suites range $199–$249. (*(800) 752-4166, gratzparkinn.com*) ❹ **Inn at Shaker Village:** The largest historic community of its kind in the country has 81 guestrooms available, including 6 suites. Located 25 miles southwest of Lexington in Pleasant Hill, the village also has a restaurant, 34 restored buildings, skilled artisans, and a slower pace of life. Guestrooms are located inside 14 of the buildings and reflect the Shaker's pared-down lifestyle. Rooms run $78–$94; suites are $94–$145. You can rent houses, too, for $170–$225. (*(800) 734-5611, shakervillageky.org*) ❺ **Kentucky Horse Park Campground:** It offers 260 sites with electric and water hookups. But it doesn't offer sewer

hookups; instead there are two dump stations. It's close to downtown, the pads are paved, and the park is pet friendly, with plenty of activities on-site. This place is popular; you must make reservations if you want a spot. Sites are $27. (*(800) 370-6416, x 257, kyhorsepark. com/khp/campground*)

❻ **Lyndon House Bed & Breakfast:** Located in downtown Lexington, this 1880s brick home is an example of a more tasteful, restrained Victorian style and has three guest rooms and two suites. The parlor and dining room have been carefully maintained with their original plaster walls, white oak floors, cherry woodwork, and ornate crown molding installed in 1883. All but one guestroom have a private bath. Rooms run $129–$239. (*(800) 494-9597, lyndonhouse.com*)

Where to Eat

TAILGATE SUPPLIES: ❶ **Good Foods Market & Café:** There are two locations— the original **Good Foods Market** on Southland Drive, and **Good Foods Chapter 2** inside the downtown Lexington Public Library. This is a locally owned and operated cooperative supermarket that carries everything you'd expect, with a focus on natural, organic, and whole foods. There's also a café, and they cater if you'd rather they do your tailgate cooking. (*(859) 278-1813, goodfoods.coop*)

SPORTS BARS: ❷ **High Life Lounge:** You can watch the game on one of their 14 plasma TVs, and you can play a game of darts, shoot some pool, or try your hand at air hockey or foosball. High Life has 26 beers on draft, plus 30 more in bottles, and pizza is the specialty (although they have a lot of deli sandwiches, too). On weekends local bands take the stage. (*$, (859) 455-8890, highlifeloungeky.com*) ❸ **Two Keys Tavern:** This cavernous room of brick and rough pine is slung with beer swag and UK paraphernalia. Be sure to look up: the ceiling's been covered with doors—odd but cool. The place also hosts live music, comedy, televised sports events, and pep rallies for Lexington's arena football team . . . just not all at once. (*$, (859) 254-5000*)

RESTAURANTS: ❹ **Jonathan at Gratz Park:** Attached to the Gratz Park Inn, this restaurant is hip and upscale. Jonathan's food has been written up in *Bon Appetit*, *Conde Nast Traveler*, and *Southern Living*, among others. Dinner will cost you some money, but lunch can be a bargain—it's nearly the same menu, but for about 40 percent less. (*$$, (859) 252-4949, jagp.info*) ❺ **Natasha's Café:** For a little something bohemian, park yourself here. The interior is a large, airy, loft-like space with tables sometimes decorated with 4-foot-tall sunflowers sitting

in improbably small glass vases. The food is inexpensive and international, with a little emphasis toward Russian dishes. At night, pierced Moroccan lanterns throw out spangled beams of candlelight. (*$, (888) 901-8412, beetnik.com*)

❻   **Tolly-Ho Restaurant:** Known as "the Ho," this UK favorite is one of Lexington's best places for great, greasy-spoon fare (including breakfast) anytime of day or night. While it's definitely popular with the college crowd, the Ho is also a favorite with locals of all stripes. There's not much in the way of atmosphere, though, just an interior with wood walls and lots of tables, plus some art on the walls. (*$, (859) 253-2007, tolly-ho.com*)

Daytime Fun

❶ **Explorium of Lexington:** This is Lexington's hands-on children's museum where kids can enjoy exhibits like Brainzilla, The Bubble Zone, and dinosaurs like Tyrannosaurus Rex and Triceratops. The exhibits and activities are designed to inspire imagination and curiosity. (*$, (859) 258-3256, explorium.com*)

❷ **Kentucky Horse Park:** You're in the heart of horse country here, so pay your respects by visiting this 1,200-plus-acre, equine-themed park and horse farm. The park offers two museums, acres of pasture, and live demonstrations with various breeds of horses. While you're here, take the 10–12 minute narrated trolley tour of activities, pulled by a team of Draft horses. There are daily shows featuring a parade of different breeds and retired champion racehorses, plus films, art, and historic exhibits. Horse rides are also available. (*$–$$, (859) 233-4303, kyhorsepark.com*) ❸ **Shaker Village at Pleasant Hill:** This is a living museum with 2,800 acres of preserved farmland, miles of trails, limestone paths, and buildings of brick and stone. As you walk through the village, you can talk with costumed interpreters who'll explain life in a 19th-century Shaker community. If you visit before the end of October, you'll be able to see farmhands plowing and working with horses and oxen, raising heirloom varieties of vegetables and grain, milking cattle, and tending sheep. You can eat lunch or dinner here; reservations are recommended for all meals. (*$$, (800) 734-5611, shakervillageky.org*) ❹ **Woodford Reserve Distillery:** They don't just raise horses around here. They make whiskey, too. Located in nearby Versailles, the distillery has been running since 1812, making it one of the oldest working distilleries in Kentucky. The "Corn to Cork" tour gives you an in-depth look at how they do it from the 14-foot-tall cypress fermenting tanks full of bubbling sour mash, through the bourbon making process, to Warehouse C, an enormous limestone warehouse from the 1880s, where the bourbon will spend years aging. Yes, you do get to sample—if you're 21 or older. Yes, you do have to prove it. (*$, (859) 879-1812, woodfordreserve.com*)

Nighttime Fun

❶ **Club Avio:** Spreading through several buildings, this complex offers more entertainment options than you have fingers . . . on both hands. For dancing, there's **Club Paragon** with a plush VIP section and multiple bars. For live music, the **Verve** concert hall hosts a variety of local and national talent every weekend. There's also a rooftop Karaoke lounge, a sand volleyball court, and a sports bar called **Lex's Pub** and **Martini Bar**. And I'm just hitting some high points here. Cover charges vary. (*$–$$, (859) 231-7263, clubavio.com*) ❷ **Comedy Off Broadway:** National touring acts take the stage here. Among the comics who've played at Off Broadway are Jerry Seinfeld, Paula Poundstone, Elayne Boosler, and Jeff Foxworthy. There's also an open-mic night the first Tuesday of each month, if you're feeling brave—and funny. Cover charges vary a little, and there's a one-drink minimum. (*$–$$, (859) 271-JOKE (5653), comedyoffbroadway.com*) ❸ **Redmon's:** This funky, below-street-level club on West Main Street is where a lot of people come to have fun (so you better make reservations, or get here early). It's owned by honky-tonk musician Larry Redmon, who's usually the main act, though other musicians also appear from time to time. (*$, (859) 252-5802, larryredmon.com*)

Shopping

❶ **Balagula World Boutique:** Remember Natasha's Café? (See #5 in Where to Eat.) Balagula is right next door. Well, actually, it's part of the café—sort of like a funky, global, bohemian version of Cracker Barrel. What you'll find are neat (and sometimes useful) items from all over the world. (*(859) 259-0183, natashascafe.com*) ❷ **Victorian Square:** This block of 16 downtown buildings dates back to the 1880s and has held everything from saloons to an opera house. Thanks to a major renovation project in 1985, the whole block is enclosed under one roof and houses a collection of shops, galleries, restaurants, and offices. Shops include a wide variety of retail, including **The Kentucky Store's** UK memorabilia, the **Main Cross Gallery's** works by local artists, and **Savané Silver's** handmade jewelry. (*(859) 252-7575, victoriansquareshoppes.com*) ❸ **University Bookstore:** If you need UK swag, here it is. The bookstore's Wildcat Korner stocks anything you can stick a logo on and probably the best prices in town. It's located across the street from Memorial Coliseum, and if you need school supplies or a molecular biology text, they have that here, too. (*(866) 685-2583, ukbookstore.com*)

LSU

Louisiana State University: 31,234 students
Baton Rouge, LA: pop. 224,097
Tiger Stadium: seats 91,600
Colors: Purple and Gold
Nickname: Fighting Tigers
Mascot: Mike the Tiger
Phone: (225) 578-2184

Visiting RVs park in Vet Med lot, open 7 a.m. Friday. Parking is $100 per game, not per day. There's overflow RV parking at Farr Park, 2 miles south of campus. Call (225) 769-7805 to make arrangements. Tailgating starts as early as 7 a.m. game day and continues until 2 hours after game. All tailgating areas are within walking distance of the stadium. No tents larger than 10 x 10 feet allowed; all music must be turned off by midnight pregame, and by 2 a.m. postgame. No portable generators allowed and no cookers larger than a 55-gallon drum.

Shuttle Info: All parking within easy walking distance. No shuttles needed.

Fighting Tigers Media Partner: 98.1-FM WDGL

Louisiana State University and Agricultural & Mechanical College was founded in the early 1800s as a military school. This tradition is still woven into the university's fabric via the school's nickname: The Ole War Skule (not to be confused with the team's nickname, Fighting Tigers).

The university had to shut down a couple of times during the Civil War, and it burned in 1869, but once rebuilt (and renamed simply Louisiana State University in 1870), it has grown into one of the country's best-known schools with one of the nation's most successful football programs.

Football came to Baton Rouge in 1893. The season lasted one game: a loss to Tulane. It's a rivalry that continues today.

But since then the Fighting Tigers have produced some of football's top players (including Y. A. Tittle and 1959 Heisman Trophy winner Billy Cannon), a dozen conference championships, and two national championships (1958 and 2003).

But the most famous LSU football moment is, arguably, the Earthquake Game, and the fault line was the Auburn defense.

Auburn was visiting LSU on October 8, 1988, and with 1:47 left in the game, LSU found itself losing 6–0 and facing a 4th and 10 on the Auburn 11. Quarterback Tommy Hodson took the snap, dropped back, and completed a pass to Eddie Fuller in the end zone. The kick made it 7–6 LSU, and the Fighting Tigers won. The crowd of 70,431 erupted so loudly that the nearby Howe-Russell Geoscience Complex's seismograph registered it as an earthquake.

School Mascot

The roots of the Fighting Tiger nickname for LSU go back to the Civil War. A Louisiana volunteer company was nicknamed the Tiger Rifles and became a part of a larger battalion that took on the nickname. The name was later applied to all of the Louisiana troops for Robert E. Lee's Army of Northern Virginia. The tiger symbol came from the Washington Artillery of New Orleans, which dates back to the 1830s.

Major David French Boyd fought with the Louisiana troops in Virginia and knew of the reputation of the Tiger Rifles and the Washington Artillery. After the war he became the first president of LSU and the school became the Tigers. In 1955 the name was altered to Fighting Tigers.

There is a live Bengal tiger that lives in a 15,000-square-foot habitat across the street from Tiger Stadium. The tiger in residence now is Mike V. Mike I was bought for $750 from the Little Rock Zoo in 1936 and was named Mike in honor of Mike Chambers, who was athletic director at the time.

Mike's game-day ritual is to spend pregame parked in his cage next to the opponent's locker room. Visiting players must pass Mike as they make their way into the stadium. Mike then makes his way to Tiger Stadium for a pregame ride in his cage . . . the LSU cheerleaders riding atop it. Tradition says for every growl from Mike before a football game, the Fighting Tigers will score a touchdown.

The costumed Mike that roams the sidelines on game day joined his live counterpart in the 1950s. His growl isn't nearly as intimidating or as good a predictor of touchdowns.

LSU Fight Song

"Fight for LSU"

Like Knights of old, Let's fight to hold
The glory of the Purple Gold.
Let's carry through, Let's die or do
To win the game for dear old LSU.
Keep trying for that high score;
Come on and fight,
We want some more, some more.
Come on you Tigers, Fight! Fight! Fight!
For dear old L-S-U.
RAH!

Game-Day Traditions
Tiger One Village

The Village is the pregame home for LSU fans. The pregame radio show, *LSU GameDay*, is broadcast here next to a stage featuring Louisiana-based bands. There're events and contests, food and drinks, and the Tiger Gift Shop. You'll find Tiger One Village alongside Tiger Stadium outside the Maravich Center.

White Jerseys

The custom of football teams across America is for the home team to wear its colors, forcing the traveling team to wear its less-spirited white uniforms. But LSU—with the exception of a few games when the team wears purple—wears white at home. Why? Well, they've been doing it since Ike was in the White House, although the two "whites" are unrelated. In 1958 the Tigers wore white at home and won the national championship. The home-whites seemed lucky, so they've been wearing them ever since, including the 2003 championship year.

Visiting LSU

Baton Rouge is the capital of Louisiana and, due to the population loss of post-Katrina New Orleans, the state's largest city. Some call it by its English translation, Red Stick, but not many; everyone calls it home to great Cajun and Creole food and lifestyles.

Where to Stay

❶ **The Cook Hotel:** This alumni-owned hotel and conference center is located on LSU's campus. You can't get any more convenient than that. Inside you'll find 74 guestrooms and 54 suites, plus two business centers and an exercise room. Rooms are $130 during football weekends; suites are $170. (*(225) 383-2665, thecookhotel.com*) ❷ **Farr Park Campground & Horse Activity Center:** Located 2 miles south of LSU, next to an equestrian facility, this quiet RV campground offers 180 sites with electric and water hookups. While there's no sewer hookup, the park provides a dumping station. The best part: the city's bus service runs shuttles to and from Tiger Stadium during home games. Sites are $12. (*(225) 272-9200, brec.org*) ❸ **Great Oaks Plantation:** This antebellum home is located on a 5-acre estate, dotted with 400-year-old live oaks, azaleas, camellias, and fruit trees. There are four guestrooms, each with private bath. Instead of a full breakfast, guests are greeted with a glass of wine upon arrival, supplied with fruit juices and other drinks in their refrigerators,

ALMA MATER

Where stately oaks and broad
magnolias shade inspiring halls,
There stands our dear old Alma Mater
who to us recalls
Fond memories that waken in our
hearts a tender glow
And make us happy for the love that
we have learned to know.
All praise to thee, our Alma Mater,
molder of mankind.
May greater glory, love unending,
be forever thine.
Our worth in life will be thy worth,
we pray to keep it true,
And may thy spirit live in us . . .
forever, L-S-U.

and offered either fresh fruits or pastries in the morning. Rooms run $145–$240. (*(225) 927-8414, greatoaksplantation.com*) ❹ **Hilton Baton Rouge Capitol Center:** I know, I'm breaking my rule a bit, but this was an independent hotel for years before Hilton spent $60 million renovating it. It's also the former home of Huey "Kingfish" Long, Louisiana's infamous governor, so I have to include it. The hotel has a restaurant, a private dining room, and a wine cellar—once the infamous tunnel Long used to sneak to and from the King Hotel. Rooms run $199–$229; suites range $350–$800. (*(877) 862-9800, hiltoncapitol center.com*) ❺ **Myrtles Plantation:** If you're driving down from the north, stop in St. Francisville and stay at this infamous 210-year-old home. The Myrtles has a reputation of being haunted—really haunted—by several very active spirits. Guests have reported hearing invisible children playing, seeing figures walk through rooms, and so on. Regardless, this B&B has 11 rooms (including 2 suites and a cottage), most with private baths. A restaurant is located on the premises, along with a large brick courtyard and gift shop. A tour is included in the room rates (not sure if a ghost is actually your guide), which range from $115–$230. (*(225) 635-6277, myrtlesplantation.com*) ❻ **Stockade Bed & Breakfast:** Located near LSU, this Spanish-style hacienda has six guestrooms, each with a private bath (except for the Blue and Red Suite that consists of adjoining rooms that share a bath). During game weekends, rates are $155 for a standard room, $235 for the Blue and Red Suite. (*(888) 900-5430, thestockade.com*)

Where to Eat

TAILGATE SUPPLIES: ❶ **Jerry Lee's Kwik Stop:** I'm sending you here for one reason: Jerry Lee's stocks the best homemade boudin sausage in town. Seasoned just right and not too greasy, their boudin has a loyal following, some of whom make road trips just for the sausage. Otherwise, Jerry Lee's is a perfectly nice little convenience store, minus the gas station. (*(225) 272-0739*)
❷ **The Main Street Market and Red Stick Farmers' Market:** Located at the government parking garage on Main Street between Fourth and Fifth Streets, these two markets can supply you with treats you didn't know you needed. Main Street Market, an indoor market offering pecan pralines, hot sauces, and other snacks lies inside the parking deck, while the Farmers' Market sets up shop outside. On rainy days, the markets are held in the Galvez Parking Garage at 500 Main Street. (*(225) 336-9532*)

SPORTS BARS: ❸ Ivar's Sports Bar & Grill: This place has its own sense of fun and energy, and patrons come to enjoy its character and happy mob. With plenty of TVs and tons of sports memorabilia, it's clear that Ivar's caters to sports fans. And they come—in large groups on game days—for the atmosphere, as well as the burgers, pizza, and wings. (*$, (225) 388-0021*) ❹ The Station Sports Bar & Grill: More than 20 TVs, many of them HD plasma TVs, ensure everybody sees the game. Now, this is not a big place, so on game day it's packed to the rafters with fans yelling "Geaux Tigers!" and enthusiastically enjoying The Station's huge list of bottled beers and premium spirits. The Station swears it has the largest collection of sports memorabilia in town. (*$, (225) 926-0631, stationsportsbar.com*)

RESTAURANTS: ❺ Boutin's Cajun Restaurant: On the outside, Boutin's is nothing special—just a huge wooden shack with a low porch. Inside, you'll find down-home Cajun cooking, like crawfish étouffée, grilled alligator, jambalaya, and lesser-known treats like corn maque choux. This isn't tourist food. Feed the fish and turtles from the back deck; there's a gumball machine of fish food. Live bands play Cajun music almost every night. (*$, (225) 819-9862, boutins.com*)

⑥ **Juban's:** It's been a hit since they opened in 1983. This casual-upscale Creole restaurant started as a series of small, cozy dining rooms surrounding a brick-paved atrium bar. They've expanded since then and offer a menu of Creole dishes that blend French, African, and Spanish traditions. (*$$, (225) 346-8422, jubans.com*) **❼ Mike Anderson's Seafood Restaurant & Oyster Bar:** Owned by the former LSU All-American linebacker, Anderson's started as a humble sandwich shop in 1975. Today there are three locations, with 60 menu selections. Local waters provide all the seafood in Anderson's dishes. The restaurant is close to LSU and popular, so expect a wait on game days, or get there early. (*$–$$, (225) 766-7823, mikeandersons.com*)

Daytime Fun

❶ Baton Rouge Zoo: More than 1,800 animals are showcased here, Baton Rouge's most popular family attraction. The zoo is home to everything from native Louisianan species to elephants, parrots, zebras, tigers, otters, and giraffes. Other attractions include train rides, a playground, café, gift shop, and petting zoo. (*$, (225) 775-3877, brzoo.org*) **❷ Magnolia Mound Plantation:** This

authentically restored 1792 French Creole plantation house, complete with outbuildings and gardens, is one of the oldest wooden structures in the state, sitting fully 5 feet off the ground. What makes it worth visiting, aside from its striking beauty, are tours that include information about how the other half—the plantation's slaves and servants—lived. (*$, (225) 343-4955, brec.org, search Park Directory*)

❸ **Swamp Tour:** Alligator Bayou, a 13,000-acre wildlife habitat 15 minutes west of Baton Rouge, offers eco-swamp tours of the Spanish Lake Basin and Bluff Swamp. Highlights along the tour include a beautiful lake of old-growth cypress trees, a moss-draped alligator swamp, a 700-year-old cypress tree with 5-foot-tall "knees," and an impressive amount of wildlife. Expect to see any of the following: snakes, turtles, black bear, deer, almost 300 species of birds, and of course, alligators. Swamp tours are available by reservation. (*$$–$$$, (225) 642-8297, alligatorbayou.com*)

Nighttime Fun

❶ **Red Star:** It's small; it's hip; it's popular with LSU students. Red Star is where you go to hang out and meet people. If it gets crowded, there's an outside deck. (*$, (225) 346-8454, redstarbar.com*) ❷ **The Roux House:** It's full of live jazz and blues with some funk and zydeco tossed into the mix. Hear it all in this cozy, hip club where weathered brick walls sport gilt-framed mirrors. Roux also serves some Cajun food and has a full bar. Try a seat upstairs in their plush martini bar. (*$, (225) 344-2583, profile.myspace.com/rouxhouse*) ❸ **The Varsity Theatre:** Situated near LSU's north gates, the Varsity is where the big acts, like Better Than Ezra, Aaron Neville, Concrete Blonde, and other Grammy-winning artists, play. Other nights Varsity morphs into a dance party, with retro and Latin music. It also turns into a sports bar on Monday nights, with a 15-foot HDTV. And on LSU game days, the place is simply insane. (*$, (225) 383-7018, varsitytheatre.com*) ❹ **Churchill's Cigars and Elixers:** In the front it's a store, where you can buy a Fuente, Davidoff, Montecristo, or any of several dozen brands of handmade cigars from a walk-in humidor. In the back, settle into a leather couch and sip an aged port, single malt Scotch. or cognac in Churchill's intimate lounge. (*$–$$, (225) 927-4211, wine-cigars.com*)

Shopping

❶ **The Historic Merchant's District:** For a selection of independent, cool shops and boutiques, travel down to Perkins Road and browse through a dozen different shops and galleries. Among the neat shops is **Cottonwood Books**, a

small, cozy store with books stacked nearly to the ceiling. **Keeper's Antiques**, just off Perkins on Hollydale Avenue, stocks antique furniture and clocks, collectibles, art by Southern artists, and unique accessories. Some of their stuff is treasure; some of it's trash; all of it's fun. **Cork and Bottle Fine Wines** offers one of the city's finest selection of wines, French, German, Italian, Greek, and domestic vintages. ❷ **The Shelton Gift Shop:** This is LSU memorabilia headquarters—well, one of them. Located inside the Cook Conference Center and Hotel, the gift shop has LSU's logo, colors, or mascot all over just about everything. (*(225) 383-0241, lsualumni.org*) ❸ **Tiger Mania:** This is the other headquarters for LSU gear. They stock pretty much everything, except lingerie. (*(225) 769-7303, collegegear.com*)

OLE MISS

University of Mississippi: 16,498 students
Oxford, MS: pop. 13,618
Vaught-Hemingway Stadium: seats 60,580
Colors: Cardinal Red and Navy Blue
Nickname: Rebels
Mascot: Officially none; Colonel Reb (traditional)
Phone: (662) 915-7167

Traveling RVs arrive 5 p.m. Friday and park free in three non-reserved areas—intramural fields off Hawthorne Road (gated entrance behind Gillom Sports Center), gravel lot at corner of Old Taylor Road and Highway 6, and Food Management Institute parking lot off Hill Drive. Tailgating at The Grove starts 12 a.m. Saturday, ends 12 a.m. Sunday. No tent stakes, no generators, no open flames of any kind, no propane grills, no alcohol.

Shuttle Info: All parking within easy walking distance. No shuttles needed.

Rebels Media Partner: 1450-AM WCJU

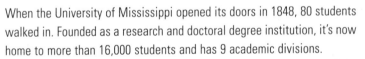

When the University of Mississippi opened its doors in 1848, 80 students walked in. Founded as a research and doctoral degree institution, it's now home to more than 16,000 students and has 9 academic divisions.

The school shut down for a period during the Civil War when most of the student body—and many of the faculty—joined the Confederate Army (although the School of Medicine remained open as a hospital for the war wounded). Their company was nicknamed the University Greys, and they suffered severe casualties during the war, including the Battle of Gettysburg when they made their deepest advance into Union territory. Only one member of the University Greys was able to come back to Ole Miss to speak to the student body.

But it wasn't Ole Miss then. That moniker comes from Elma Meek's

winning entry in an 1896 contest to name a new student publication. As it turned out she ended up renaming the school. Over time Ole Miss became the school's nickname and then its primary name used today by students, alumni, fans, and broadcasters covering the school's teams. The school's football team had been around for about 3 years when Elma penned the Ole Miss name.

The father of Mississippi football is Dr. A. L. Bondurant, the graduate school dean who organized the school's athletic association in 1890 and coached its first football team in 1893. Ole Miss got off to a good start—a 56–0 trouncing of Southwest Baptist University.

In its first years the coaching position was a volunteer one, and a revolving door. From Bondurant's debut until 1925, there were 22 coaches and only 7 of them coached more than one season. If you need a cocktail party trivia question, the first paid coach was C. D. Clark in 1894.

But the name most associated with the Rebels football program is "Manning." Archie Manning was a star quarterback for Ole Miss in the 1960s; his senior year he finished third in the Heisman Trophy balloting. He married a former Ole Miss homecoming queen, and one of their sons, Eli, followed in his father's footsteps as quarterback for the Rebels—leading the team in 2003 to its first 10-win season in

30 years. (Another Manning son, Peyton, starred at SEC rival Tennessee.)

If you doubt Archie Manning's impact on Ole Miss, just take a drive around campus. The speed limit is 18. That was Archie's jersey number.

School Mascot

In 1936 the student newspaper, the *Mississippian*, held a contest for a school nickname. More than 200 names were entered, including "Rebels" by Judge Ben Guider. It was one of five finalists sent to journalists for their votes. Twenty-one writers responded and 18 of them voted for "Rebels."

Another judge, and University Athletic Committee chairman, William Hemingway, upon seeing the choice said, "If 18 sports writers wish to use Rebels, I shall not rebel, so let it go Ole Miss Rebels."

Two years later the school yearbook was published as *The Rebel Number* and along with it the illustration of Colonel Reb, who was designed to resemble the ideal of the Southern Gentleman. In 1979, Colonel Reb took human form as a costumed mascot for Ole Miss, and he roamed the sidelines until 2003.

That was when university administrators, saying the mascot didn't represent anything the school does, eliminated Colonel Reb and held a contest to replace him.

The finalists that fans were asked to vote for were Rebel Bruiser and Rowdy Rebel. The lack of votes and ridicule of the decision led to the cancellation of the vote. As a result, Ole Miss does not officially have a mascot.

The decision is still unpopular with many students and alumni. The Colonel Reb Foundation is leading the effort to reinstate the traditional mascot and is now the largest student group on campus.

Game-Day Traditions
The Grove and The Walk of Champions

There is no bigger or more honored tradition at Ole Miss than tailgating. Sure, other schools do it . . . but not like this.

When stepping onto the 10 acres of oak tree–shaded grass in the middle of campus known as The Grove, you can be forgiven if you think you've walked into a charity fund-raiser. Men in jackets and ties, women in dresses—some are dressed to the nines, others more comfortably, but all are dressed to be seen.

So are their tailgate setups: tables set with china, silver, and centerpieces; cocktails and appetizers served before entrées. This is more than a tailgate party: it's a cocktail and dinner party. It's also a reunion for scores of fans who have attended Ole Miss and tailgated at The Grove for generations.

Tailgating at The Grove is like tailgating nowhere else. *Sports Illustrated* has named Ole Miss the nation's top tailgating school. *The Sporting News* has called The Grove "the Holy Grail of tailgating sites." Tents start popping up in the dark at midnight Friday before home games, and the last ones aren't packed up until Sunday.

The atmosphere and tradition of The Grove is so powerful that in 1983 Ole Miss Coach Billy Brewer wanted his players to be able to experience it. They couldn't set up tents and grills, of course, so instead, 2 hours before kickoff, Coach Brewer walked his team from the athletic dorm to the stadium through The Grove. He took a different route each week, until 1985 when he picked a permanent route along a sidewalk that runs through the heart of The Grove.

Fans lined up on either side of the sidewalk to greet the players with cheers and encouragement. Three years later, thanks to a gift from the unbeaten 1962 Rebels team, the Walk of Champions arch was erected and now is where the team begins its walk through The Grove on home-game days, still flanked by cheering fans.

Hotty Toddy

You'll hear this chant from Ole Miss fans, but no one is really sure where it came from, and they aren't talking about a drink. Or maybe they are.

"Forward Rebels"

Forward Rebels, march to fame,
Hit that line and win this game,
We know that you'll fight it through,
For your colors Red and Blue
Rah, Rah, Rah.
Rebels, you're the Southland's pride,
Take that ball and hit your stride,
Don't stop 'till the victory's won
For your Ole Miss.
Fight, fight for your Ole Miss.

The cheer's origin is good fodder for Ole Miss Internet forums and message boards. There are three fairly popular legends you'll find about the chant. The thing they have in common is that it was created by students in the 1930s.

One story has it that, at a game up north, a group of students was cold and drinking hot toddies. Apparently they drank enough of them that they decided to honor their beverage with a cheer, and it caught on.

Another has it that a different group of students created Hotty Toddy as a mocking version of the phrase "hoity toity" in response to Ole Miss students and alumni being called that by fans of rival schools.

The third legend is that the cheer is a Southernized version of an old soldier chant. Propagators of this theory point to the show *Band of Brothers* when the characters were training in Georgia. Members of EZ Company, they will tell you, were yelling, "Highty Tighty, Gosh a mighty, Who in the hell are we?" as they ran up a hill in the show's first episode.

Pick the story you like and go with it . . . just get the words right when reciting the chant. Here they are to help you out:

Are you ready? Hell yes! Damn Right!
Hotty Toddy, Gosh almighty
Who in the hell are we? Hey!
Flim Flam, Bim Bam,
Ole Miss, By Damn!

Visiting Ole Miss

In 1835 three businessmen built a log cabin and a general store on a hill in Lafayette County. A town was born. One of the men's nephew suggested they name the town Oxford, after the city in England whose name is better known as one of the world's best universities. His wish was that someday Mississippi would open the state's first public university here. Wishes can come true, and that university is what life in this small town revolves around.

ALMA MATER

Way down south in Mississippi
There's a spot that ever calls
Where amongst the hills enfolded
Stand old Alma Mater's Halls
Where the trees lift high their branches
To the whispering Southern breeze
There Ole Miss is calling, calling
To our hearts fond memories.

Where to Stay

❶ **Blue Creek Cabin:** On a lush 50-acre spread about 10 minutes from town, this rustic,1880s log cabin has two guest bedrooms (one king and one queen), a family room with a wood-burning fireplace, and hand-carved furniture and

Prime Real Estate

Inn at Ole Miss: Located on the Ole Miss campus, directly across from The Grove, this 91-room inn is the best place in town to stay for football weekends. But you never will. It's sold out for about the next 30 years. Faithful alumni buy these rooms outright for football weekends and then bequeath them to their next of kin. The inn is currently expanding, adding a tower with 40 two-room suites, a large ballroom, an exercise facility, and a café. Don't even think about it. It's already sold out, too. If you really want to stay here, come for a baseball game or something. They have plenty of rooms available then. ((662) 234-2331, theinnatolemiss.com/new)

antiques. The single bathroom has a rare, handmade copper bathtub, along with separate shower and hand-carved vanity. The cabin's kitchenette has a working, hand-operated water pump (I told you it was rustic). There's satellite TV, but no telephone service; although most cell phones do get service. During football weekends the cabin rents for $700 (it's $550 other times of the year). ((662) 238-2897, bluecreek cabin.com) ❷ **Campground at Barnes Crossing:** It's about an hour's drive from Oxford, but this is the best overnight RV spot in the area. Barnes Crossing has 40 sites with full hookups, cable TV, and telephone and modem hookups. Most sites are very shady with nice landscaping. There's a manager on duty around-the-clock, and the campground also has security. Sites are $25. ((662) 844-6063, cgbarnescrossing.com) ❸ **The Colonel's Quarters:** About 5 miles outside of town, this Greek revival house comes with four guest rooms, all with private baths. While the first floors of the house are furnished in a very formal, period fashion, guestrooms have an earthier feeling, with wood-paneled walls and a mixture of antique and modern furnishings. Rooms run $69–$149. ((662) 236-9601, thecolonelsquarters.com) ❹ **Downtown Oxford Inn & Suites:** Within walking distance of the Courthouse Square, this recently renovated hotel is close to dining, shopping, and Ole Miss. The hotel has rooms and suites that, during football weekends, run from $179 to $249. ((662) 234-3031, downtownoxfordinnandsuites.com) ❺ **The Tree House Bed & Breakfast:** This unique log home has seven guest rooms, all with private baths. Situated on 5 wooded acres, this B&B is 4 miles from Ole Miss. The house's outdoor pool, hot tub, and gazebo are open for guests year-round. Rooms are $105–$130, based on what day of the week you're here. (*(877) 849-8738, thetreehousebandb.com*)

Where to Eat

TAILGATE SUPPLIES: ❶ **Good Earth Gourmet Market:** This is a new store that specializes in organic produce and meats from local and regional growers, as well as baby foods. The market also stocks pet and personal care products, and products for the home. You can even find unique handmade gifts for sale. (*(662) 234-3300*)

SPORTS BARS: ❷ **The Library Sports Bar:** Just call it the "Sports Bar" and everyone will know where you're talking about. Located on the corner of 11th Street and Van Buren—just down the street from its parent, the Library Bar & Grill—it fills the void of a true sports bar on the Oxford Square. Inside you can watch the game on any of 11 TVs, including 1 huge projection screen. (*$, (662) 234-1411*)

RESTAURANTS: ❸ **Abner's Famous Chicken Tenders:** You like sports. You like food. Chances are you're going to like this sports restaurant. Now a small chain with locations in Mississippi and the Memphis area, this is the original, started by former Ole Miss football player Abner White. Abner's has wall-to-wall sports memorabilia and a menu featuring chicken tenders (of course), wraps, salads, baked potatoes, and other side items. (*$, (662) 232-8659, abnerschicken.com*)

❹ **Downtown Grill:** One of Oxford's best restaurants, the Grill serves upscale New-Southern cuisine such as catfish Lafitte with sautéed gulf shrimp, julienne ham, and spicy cream sauce. The restaurant is located in a restored building on the city's historic square downtown, but the name gave that away. There's also an upstairs bar with a balcony and a nice view. On football weekends reservations are essential. (*$$, (662) 234-2659, downtowngrill.net*) ❺ **The Rib Cage:** This could also fit in the Sports Bars category, since it's a rib joint with an upstairs restaurant and downstairs sports bar. You can catch a game on one of their 10 TVs and enjoy a slab of ribs at the same time. The draft beer also keeps the crowd coming in. (*$, (662) 238-2929*) ❻ **Yocona River Inn:** About 9 miles east of Oxford, you'll find an old general store. Don't let the exterior fool you. Inside is some good, upscale food. Locals suggest ordering the filet with its tasty crust and red wine sauce. The rest of the menu changes weekly. It's Brown Bag, so BYOB if you want alcohol. Yocona doesn't take reservations, and they often quit taking names by 7 p.m. on Fridays during football weekends, so get here early. On the bright side, diners tailgate on the porch while waiting for a table. (*$$, (662) 234-2464, yocona.com*)

Daytime Fun

❶ **Holly Springs National Forest:** This 155,000-acre forest offers recreational opportunities from mild to wild, including some of the best fishing lakes in the state, nature trails, picnic areas, and campgrounds. Parts of Holly Springs were created in the 1930s by the Civilian Conservation Corps in order to reclaim land depleted by cotton farming. Today, the forest includes stands of loblolly pines, bottomland hardwoods, and restored wetlands rich in wildlife. (*$, (662) 236-6550, fs.fed.us/r8/mississippi/hollysprings*) ❷ **Ole Miss Blues Archive:** On the third floor of the John Davis Williams Library, in the Department of Archives and Special Collections, lies the Mecca of recorded blues. The Blues Archive houses one of the world's largest collections of blues recordings, publications, and memorabilia. There are thousands of pictures, videos, books, and

periodicals, and more than 50,000 sound recordings. B. B. King even recorded a live album (*Live at Ole Miss*) in The Grove. (*Free, (662) 915-7753, olemiss.edu/ depts/general_library/files/archives*) ❸ **Rowan Oak:** Just blocks off the square, this stately house sits at the end of a long, cedar-lined drive. This was William Faulkner's home, where he wrote his Nobel Prize–winning novels. Faulkner even wrote part of a novel on the wall of his bedroom, later uncovered during a renovation. Rowan Oak was Faulkner's private world, in reality and imagination. Fresh from an extensive renovation, the house is preserved just as he left it— except for the museum-quality climate control. They added that. (*$, (662) 234-3284, olemiss.edu/depts/u_museum/ rowan_oak/interactive.html*)

Nighttime Fun

❶ **The Longshot:** The bar's rough, plaster walls are sunset red, with a long wooden bar and a reputation for booking great bands. You'll hear some Mississippi legends on the bar's narrow stage, like roots rocker Cary Hudson and Mississippi bluesman T-Model Ford. A local favorite is Wiley and the Checkmates, fronted by 61-year-old Herbert Wiley. He runs a shoe repair shop and has a fondness for spangled jumpsuits and James Brown theatrics. (*$, (662)*

236-7063, thelongshotbar.com) ❷ **Proud Larry's:** By day it's a great place for hand-tossed pizza, pastas, salads, and burgers. By night, it becomes an Oxford hotspot featuring great live music, including local and regional bands—like the Dirty Dozen Brass Band—as well as occasional surprises, such as Elvis Costello. Proud Larry's is known for booking literate rock one night and a hippie jam band the next. Cover charges vary. (*$–$$, (662) 236-0050, proudlarrys.com*) ❸ **The Thacker Mountain Radio Show:** If you're in town on Thursday night, you can catch this weekly live radio show that takes over a local bookstore, creating an eclectic program that's part *Austin City Limits*, part *Prairie Home Companion*. Each week the show features the Thacker Mountain house band and authors like Elmore Leonard reading from and signing their latest works. There are plenty of guest musicians, too, from Elvis Costello (he sure gets around Oxford) and Gillian Welch, to international artists like Senegalese musician Guelel Kumba. Kumba was so smitten with the town after his performance, he moved here. Really. (*Free, (662) 236-2262, thackermountain.com*)

Shopping

❶ Lilly Pad: It's the perfect spot to purchase fraternity, sorority, and other personalized gifts for your favorite Ole Miss fan. You can also pick up Vera Bradley bags, candles, Burt's Bees bath products, wine bags, beaded jewelry, silver items, and picture frames. (*(662) 238-2900, lilypadgiftshop.com*)

❷ Oxford's Historic Square: For an afternoon's worth of browsing, buying, or window-shopping, hit Oxford's town square. There are several shops in the square. The South's oldest store, **Neilson's Department Store**, is here (opened in 1839), as well as places like kitchenware shop **Mississippi Madness** and **University Sporting Goods**, where you'll find plenty of Rebels gear and some tailgating supplies. Step into **Square Books**, and you'll find books on the first floor and a café on the second, with a 90-foot balcony overlooking the square. Who knows, you may run into John Grisham here; he has a law degree from Ole Miss and a house here.

MISSISSIPPI STATE

Mississippi State University: 15,934 students
Starkville, MS: pop. 21,869
Davis Wade Stadium at Scott Field: seats 55,082
Colors: Maroon and White
Nickname: Bulldogs
Mascot: Bully
Phone: (662) 325-8121

RVs park as early as noon Friday in non-reserved lots on Stone Boulevard, past Spring Street/Blackjack Road. RVs vacate by 7 a.m. Sunday or 7 a.m. the next day of classes. RVs pay $40 for weekend passes, available on-site. Cars pay $5 or $10 in lots near Bully Boulevard, Dudy Noble Field, and adjacent to unreserved RV lots. Other lots are free. Tailgating starts as early as 5 p.m. Friday for weekend or holiday games and 5 hours before weekday games. Don't park on grass or obstruct traffic or parking areas. Tents limited to 12 x 12 feet. No tents, tables, or chairs in parking spaces or on sidewalks. Charcoal grills allowed. Follow state and local laws on alcohol. Picnic areas in Picnic Zone are first-come, first-served.

Shuttle Info: Free shuttle service available from Thad Cochran Research and Economic Development Park north of Hwy 182 from campus. Shuttles will run 2 hours prior to game time and continue until 2 hours after game's end.

Bulldogs Media Partner: 107.9-FM WFCA

A land-grant college, The Agricultural and Mechanical College of the State of Mississippi was created by the state legislature in 1878, accepting its first students 2 years later. Its mission was to offer training in agriculture and mechanical arts, of course, without forgetting other

studies, "including military tactics," which was a requirement of land-grant schools.

Of course, over time the school had its mission expanded, and with it, in 1932, the state changed the school's name from Mississippi A&M to Mississippi State College, and later, in 1958, it was renamed Mississippi State University.

It was Mississippi A&M that kicked off the school's football legacy in 1892, although it was a bit different from the start of football at most schools: it was the faculty versus the students. The first game was a 4–0 faculty win, the first of an undefeated season for the teachers.

The more traditional start of football was in 1895 when a team of cadets took on, and lost to, Southwestern Baptist University. The team played until 1897 when first a yellow fever scare, and then the Spanish-American War the next year, disbanded the team.

In 1901 Bulldogs football returned, but the school would wait nearly a century for its most successful teams. Those were coached by Jackie Sherrill, who walked the sidelines in Starkville from 1991–2003. While his overall coaching record at MSU was 75-75-2, he led the team to the SEC West title in 1998, coached the Bulldogs to a #12 final ranking the next year, and took his teams to six bowl games.

But perhaps his most memorable moment was his unique use of a bull during practice one year before MSU played #13 Texas. He castrated it. It worked. His unranked team toppled Texas that Saturday.

When Sherrill left Starkville in 2003, the school replaced him with a Tuscaloosa native who played for "Bear" Bryant at Alabama, winning a national title in 1973. But what was historic about the choice of Sylvester Croom as head coach was that he was the first African-American to lead a Southeastern Conference team. While acknowledging the accomplishment, Croom downplayed it saying, "I want to make sure everybody understands, I am the first African-American coach in the SEC, but there isn't but one color that matters here—and that color is Maroon."

School Mascot

The Bulldog was officially adopted as the school mascot in 1961, although the name had been used interchangeably with Aggies and Maroons during the years before. The mascot was chosen, in part, because the university felt the bulldog shared with its teams the traits of toughness and tenaciousness. Several sports writers also wrote about Mississippi State's "bulldog style" of play.

Bully is the school's live mascot. It is an AKC-registered English Bulldog. Although his ancestors were allowed to live in fraternities and wander freely through campus, the current Bully lives at the School of Veterinary Medicine.

"Hail State"

Hail dear ole State!
Fight for that victory today.
Hit that line and tote that ball,
Cross the goal before you fall!
And then we'll yell, yell, yell, yell!
For dear ole State we'll yell like H-E-L-L!
Fight for Mis-sis-sip-pi State,
Win that game today!

The guy in the bulldog costume also answers to Bully and is a part of the MSU cheerleading team.

Game-Day Traditions
Cowbells

Everyone from opponents to the SEC (which bans "artificial noise-makers") has tried to silence MSU's cowbells. But they still ring every game day—just not inside the stadium during conference games. The cowbells are unique to Bulldogs fans, but no one really knows how the tradition started.

While they may have gradually appeared during the 1930s and 1940s, the most popular legend is that a Jersey cow wandered onto the field one Saturday when what was then called "State College" was hosting rival Ole Miss. The Bulldogs beat the Rebels that day, and students took the cow as a good luck charm . . . so much so they continued to bring a cow to games for a while. Eventually they

realized bringing just the cowbell was easier, so it came to represent the cow and good luck.

The cowbells grew in popularity in the 1950s, and in the 1960s they became a school symbol. That was also when they began welding handles on the bells, making them easier to ring and louder.

In 1974 the SEC banned the cowbells from inside the stadium, calling them a disruption. But you can still hear them clearly as fans outside ring them in celebration. Those fans do take their bells inside for nonconference games.

Visiting Mississippi State

While most people have always associated Starkville with Mississippi State, in 1969 there were a lot of people who associated it with Johnny Cash. He was arrested here for public drunkenness, and a cut on his 1969 album *At San Quentin* was "Starkville City Jail" about his time in the city. Chances are you'll enjoy yourself more than Johnny did while visiting this small college town that prides itself on its old Southern charm.

ALMA MATER

"Maroon and White"

In the heart of Mississippi
Made by none but God's own hands
Stately in her nat'ral splendor
Our Alma Mater proudly stands.
State College of Mississippi,
Fondest mem'ries cling to thee.
Life shall hoard thy spirit ever,
Loyal sons we'll always be.

Chorus:

Maroon and White! Maroon and White!
Of thee with joy we sing.
Thy colors bright, our souls delight,
With praise our voices ring.

Tho' our life some pow'r may vanquish,
Loyalty can't be o'er run;
Honors true on thee we lavish
Until the setting of the sun;
Live Maroon and White for ever,
Ne'er can evil mar thy fame,
Nothing us from thee can sever,
Alma Mater we acclaim.

Where to Stay

❶ The Cedars: Built in 1836, this antebellum mansion is surrounded by a beautiful 183-acre estate dotted with forests, rolling pastureland, and fishing ponds just 5 minutes from MSU. Each of the four themed guestrooms comes equipped with a full bath. The mansion retains seven hand-carved fireplace mantles, ornate electric light fixtures from the early 1900s, hardware dating back to the early 1800s, and hand-poured glass. Rooms run $65 to $75. (*(662) 324-7569*)

❷ Hickory Hill: Five miles from campus, you'll find these 2 private cabins nestled in the center of 62 acres of woods and prairie land. Both cabins are about 800 square feet and resemble small, rural farmhouses, with a king bed and queen sleeper sofa, a full kitchen, and a dining and sitting area. A breakfast basket is waiting inside when you arrive. A stay in a cabin will cost you $80. (*(662) 324-2695, hickoryhill.net*) **❸ Hotel Chester:** Having first opened in 1925, it's both the oldest and newest hotel in Starkville, thanks to some extensive renovations and new ownership. While the rooms aren't hip, they are comfortable, and the hotel offers several B&B-like touches, such as a free, made-to-order breakfast. Rooms here run $80–$170. (*(866) 325-5005, suitedreams.cc/default.aspx*)

❹ Mississippi Horse Park: Located just south of campus, this 100-acre facility has an RV park with 47 sites available. Each site has water and electric hookups, and a dump station is located on the grounds. There are also numerous electric-only spots around each of the three horse barns. Sites are $15 on football weekends. (*(662) 325-9350, msucares.com/centers/agricenter/index.html*)

Where to Eat

TAILGATE SUPPLIES: ❶ **Gour Mae's Grocery:** Located in the Cotton District neighborhood, this specialty food and neighborhood market sells Mississippi-created products like cheese-straws, sauces, and dips, along with imported products from around the world. You can have them put together a basket of items for your tailgate party, too. If you need beer, try Lazy Magnolia (made in Mississippi) in a "party pig," about a case worth's of beer with a self-contained tap. There are several flavors including Blue Heron and Southern Pecan. (*(662) 323-3030, gourmae.com*)

SPORTS BARS: ❷ **The Boar's Head:** This outdoor tiki bar on University Drive is the place to hang out on game day. With planted palms swaying and MSU's fight song playing on the sound system, it's hard not to feel the school spirit. TVs ring the hut, while fans ring the bar. There's a covered stage for live bands and a drink called the Pickled Pig that's a house specialty. (*$, (662) 324-6329,*

myspace.com/theboarshead) ❸ **The Dawghouse Lounge:** Located inside The Veranda restaurant, the Dawghouse is one of the most popular places to watch a game in Starkville—at least on TV. And the lounge has a big 50-inch plasma one. Their menu isn't your normal sports-bar food; try the wild sockeye salmon or the Kobe burger. (*$–$$, (662) 323-1231, verandastarkville.com*) ❹ **The Grill:** The Grill is a favorite with alums who return for games and to visit the old stomping grounds. The Grill has upscale pub fare for both appetizers and meals, such as skewers of filet mignon or Gulf shrimp. You'll watch the game on 1 of the bar's 11 TVs, or its 6-foot projection screen. MSU jerseys hang on the walls next to plaques honoring victorious college bowl games and mementoes from bands that have performed here. (*$–$$, (662) 323-6062, eatwithus.com*)

RESTAURANTS: ❺ **Bin612:** The menu looks pretty average—until you take a closer look. They call it a Club Sandwich, but it's made with crispy pancetta and smoked provolone, then served on toasted potato bread with a roasted garlic aioli for mayo. Most of the menu has similar twists. Bin612 is set in the trademark "blue building" of Starkville's refurbished Cotton District, and its walls are decorated with work by local artists. (*$, (662) 324-6126, bin612.com*)

6 **Cappe's Steakhouse:** Cappe's serves up well-seasoned, richly flavored steaks cheap enough for a student's wallet. Locals will tell you the steaks served here are often larger than listed on the menu, but they still charge the price on the menu. (*$, (662) 324-1987*) **7** **The Little Dooey Barbeque and Blues:** They've started opening franchises and bottling their sauce, but it all started here. You can get traditional smoked and barbecued ribs and chicken, but the signature dish is the ribs that are smoked, rubbed, battered twice, then fried and served with a tomato-based sauce. Dooey's features live blues music every Friday and Saturday. (*$–$$, (662) 323-6094, thelittledooey.com*)

Daytime Fun

1 **Aspen Bay Candle Tour:** This family-owned company offers tours of its candle-making facility, where an impressive assortment of hand-poured candles are created and shipped around the world. The tour ends at their showroom and gift shop, which makes it easy to find a gift to take home. (*Free, (800) 819-7631, aspenbaycandles.com*) **2** **Golf:** The **MSU Golf Course** is regularly ranked as one of the nation's best courses by *Golf Digest* magazine and *USA Today*. Golfers say it's rare to play this PGA-sanctioned course without using every club

in your bag. Weekend fees run $24–$40. (*$$$, (662) 325-3028, golfcourse. msstate.edu/course.php*) Another popular course is **Highlands Plantation Golf Club**, a semiprivate course 2 miles away from MSU, fashioned after traditional Scottish courses with lakes, bunkers, and dramatic elevation changes. Greens fees and a cart run $40 on the weekends. (*$$$, (662) 323-7271, highlands plantationgolf.com*) ❸ **Mississippi Entomological Museum:** This is the Orkin guy's worst nightmare. The museum's bug collection has more than a million specimens on display, with thousands more added each year. Many are butterflies or moths; some from as far away as Fiji. There's also a collection of insect photographs, both unsettling and fascinating. You can take a tour, but you need to call ahead to make an appointment. (*Free, (662) 325-2990, msstate.edu /org/mississippientmuseum*)

Nighttime Fun

❶ **Dave's Darkhorse Tavern:** Listen to quirky bands; eat some deep-dish pizza. Inside the Darkhorse you won't find fancy décor: tables are made of anything from Formica to wood planks, and the walls range from brick to unpainted particle board. But they have live music six nights a week. There's also seating outside in a fenced patio. (*$, (662) 324-3316, davesdarkhorse.com*) ❷ **Remington Hunt Club:** A combination of penny drinks, live entertainment, plenty of dance floors, and a mechanical bull puts the Hunt Club on the short list of places to be at night. With numerous expansions in the last few years, the club consists of the **Coyote Concert Hall**, the **Camphouse**, and the club's original dance space. Total capacity here is 3,000, with weekend dance parties that usually draw more than 1,000 people. (*$–$$, (662) 323-2892, huntorbehunted.com*) ❸ **Rick's Café:** There's always something going on, like live music, a football game, a bikini contest, or a DJ spinning tunes. Rick's is no slouch when it comes to live music either: acts like Everclear, Maroon 5, and Kenny Chesney have played here. There's a huge outdoor tiki bar with a sand volleyball court, a brand-new blues bar upstairs, and a 20-foot TV screen. Some nights there's a cover charge, which varies according to the event. (*Free–$$, (662) 323-7425, rickscafe.net*)

Shopping

❶ **Giggleswick Village:** This is a little collection of four stores selling gifts, sweets, and other knickknacks. **Giggleswick**, the store, sells everything from Waterford Crystal and fine linens to MSU Bulldog gifts. Next door at **Wigtizzle**, you can pick up sorority gifts, accessories, and stuff for your bath . . . or

handmade chocolates and truffles. There's also **Babywick** with, you guessed it, things for babies and **Village Paper**, which sells fine stationery and invitations (guess they didn't like the name Paperwick). (*(800) 360-9336, giggleswick.com*)

❷ **The Lodge:** They sell everything imaginable with a Mississippi State logo on it, from infants' onesies to cheerleader outfits and Bulldog figurines. They've also got a tailgating corner with pretty much everything you'll need for your tailgate, except the grill. (*(800) 685-4678, yhst-29267310653951.stores. yahoo.net*)   ❸ **Old Main District:** Starkville's Main Street has become a nice shopping district, with new independent retail stores opening every day. Okay, not every day, but you will find **Iota** and **Sundial**, two separate stores sharing a single storefront space, selling local art (Iota) and eclectic clothing with a bit of a gypsy feel to it (Sundial). Down the street is **Pretties**, the top high-end boutique in town, and **Smith & Byars**, one of Starkville's oldest men's stores.

SOUTH CAROLINA

University of South Carolina: 23,722 students
Columbia, SC: pop. 117,508
Williams-Brice Stadium: seats 80,250
Colors: Garnet and Black
Nickname: Gamecocks
Mascot: Cocky
Phone: (803) 799-3387

RVs and cars park at State Fairgrounds, adjacent to stadium. (Stadium's not on campus.) Parking is close to stadium. RVs may arrive 5 p.m. Friday. Weekend parking $75 or $40 for game day only. Cars pay $15–$20 (based on proximity to stadium). Tailgating starts 7 a.m. game day, runs until midnight after game. No campfires or open flames (grills are okay). USC now has Gamecock Village, with former players signing autographs, live entertainment, games, food and beverage, USC cheerleaders, and mascot. Gamecock Village located in grandstands at State Fair Grounds, open 3 hours prior to kickoff.

Shuttle Info: All parking within easy walking distance. No shuttles needed.

Gamecocks Media Partners: 106.7-FM WTCB, 1320-AM WISW

When South Carolina College was founded, the idea was to promote harmony between the Lowcountry and the Backcountry. Harmony is not something the school's early decades were full of.

South Carolina College's first class, in 1805, had nine students. Over time the school grew in size and reputation, but shut down during the Civil War.

During Reconstruction, in 1866, the school reopened, and the rebuilding was filled with controversy and racial division. When Republicans took con-

"The Fighting Gamecocks Lead the Way"

Hey, Let's give a cheer, Carolina is here,
The Fighting Gamecocks lead the way.
Who gives a care, if the going gets tough,
And when it is rough, that's when the
'Cocks get going.
Hail to our colors of Garnet and Black,
In Carolina pride have we.
So, Go Gamecocks Go—FIGHT!
Drive for the goal—FIGHT!
USC will win today—GO COCKS!
So, let's give a cheer, Carolina is here.
The Fighting Gamecocks All The Way!

trol of the state government, they appointed two black trustees to the board, and Secretary of State Henry Hayne, a black man, enrolled in the college. Many white students, and some of the faculty, left the school, and by 1875 almost all of the student body was black.

As Reconstruction ended in 1877, the Democratic Party resumed power in South Carolina and shut down the school again. It was reopened, only to face possible closure again in 1890 when Ben Tillman was elected the state's governor. He had campaigned on the promise to shutter the school—he claimed it was elitist and didn't help the farmers—but he was unable to keep that campaign promise.

In 1906 the school was rechartered as the University of South Carolina, and its fortune turned, becoming accredited in 1917 and growing into a statewide university with campuses across the Palmetto State.

South Carolina's football history is also tied to Governor Tillman. When he was unable to shut down South Carolina, he and some others founded a college to specialize in teaching agriculture. The school: Clemson.

Thus when USC and Clemson met for the first time in 1896, what has become the third longest, uninterrupted college football rivalry (it's been uninterrupted since 1909) was already bitter. For the record, Carolina won that game 12–6.

The school has had an up-and-down football history but has never been a national power. It did win the ACC title in 1969 and has turned out some NFL stars like Sterling Sharpe and George Rogers (who won the Heisman Trophy in 1980). The school has tried to turn its team around with some high-profile coaches—first Lou Holtz and now Steve Spurrier, who has begun to pump new life into the Gamecocks.

School Mascot

For nearly a century the University of South Carolina's teams have been called the Fighting Gamecocks. You won't find another major college in America with this name.

In case you aren't familiar with cock fights (which have been outlawed for years but was a popular sport in the 19th century), a gamecock is a fighting rooster known for its feistiness, courage, and spirit—and its ability to rip other gamecocks to shreds. These birds would fight until one killed the other in front of a cheering crowd whose members usually had money on one of the birds.

South Carolina has a long history of breeding and training fighting gamecocks, and in 1900 this legacy became the moniker of the state university—replacing a slew of other less popular nicknames. The mascot you see walking the field is "Cocky," who took over mascot duties from his father, Big Spur, in 1980.

Game-Day Traditions
Cockaboose Railroad

This railroad doesn't move, but it rocks on game day.

The Cockaboose Railroad is a string of 22 cabooses that line the railroad tracks just outside Williams-Brice Stadium. The idea came from a Columbia businessman and fan who grew tired of seeing the tracks sitting nearby. So in 1990 some ultimate tailgaters began throwing their pregame parties in these well-tailored cabooses, which include running water, cable television, heat and air, and a living room. There's no tailgating like it anywhere else in the nation.

But you probably won't get to tailgate here unless you know someone. These

THE ULTIMATE TAILGATER'S SEC HANDBOOK

gems went for $40,000 originally—before they were outfitted like luxury hotels—and now are worth several times that. The railroad operates like a neighborhood association with annual fees and bylaws.

And if you do know someone and get to tailgate in one, invite me. Please.

Team Entrance

If you're in the stands for a home game, as kickoff time approaches, you'll see what the *Sporting News* has called the most exciting pregame entry in college football.

As the team leaves the locker room and gathers in the stadium tunnel, from the loud speakers comes the music from *2001: A Space Odyssey*. As the music continues, the crowd noise rises, and, in perfect timing with the music, the Gamecocks rush onto the field. More than 82,000 fans cheer as the team enters, and USC is ready to take on another foe.

ALMA MATER

"We Hail Thee, Carolina"

We hail thee, Carolina, and sing thy high praise

With loyal devotion, remembering the days

When proudly we sought thee, thy children to be:

Here's a health, Carolina, forever to thee!

Since pilgrims of learning, we entered thy walls

And found dearest comrades in thy classic halls

We've honored and loved thee as sons faithfully;

Here's a health, Carolina, forever to thee!

Generations of sons have rejoiced to proclaim

Thy watchword of service, thy beauty and fame;

For ages to come shall their rallying cry be:

Here's a health, Carolina, forever to thee!

Fair shrine of high honor and truth, thou shalt still

Blaze forth as a beacon, thy mission fulfill,

And crowned by all hearts in a new jubilee:

Here's a health, Carolina, forever to thee!

Visiting South Carolina

South Carolina's capital city, and largest, Columbia is one of America's most livable cities, too. At least that's what the folks at Partners for Livable Communities say, including Columbia on its list of 30 most livable communities. You'll find lots of cultural and recreational activities here, as well as some of the fun you'd expect near campus.

Where to Stay

❶ **Barnyard RV Park:** About 11 miles outside of town, Barnyard offers 129 sites, with full hookups and a swimming pool. Cable TV is free, but there's a charge for Wi-Fi Internet. If you're a flea market fan, the park is adjacent to the Barnyard Flea Market. Sites run $23. (*(800) 633-6351, barnyardrvpark.com*)

❷ **Chesnut Cottage Bed and Breakfast:** This home once belonged to Mary Chesnut, whose diary provided much of the emotional power in Rick Burns's *The Civil War* miniseries. Now you can sleep in one of four guestrooms—each with a private bath—in this perfectly preserved home. Located in Columbia's historic district, the cottage is within walking distance of several top restaurants and shops. Rooms run $159–$229, but during home game weekends, there may be a two-night minimum. (*(803) 256-1718, chesnutcottage.com*) ❸ **Claussen's Inn at Five Points:** Located in the Five Points district near the university, this inn delivers a lot of style and verve. Each of its 29 large guest rooms is individually decorated, with walls painted periwinkle or watermelon. Other features include Windsor chairs, pine armoires, and small patios. Complimentary wine, sherry, or brandy is served in the lobby. Rooms run from $140 for a single to $155 for a double. Suites range from $155 to $170. (*(800) 622-3382, claussensinn.com*) ❹ **The Inn at USC:** You can't get any closer to the action. This 117-room hotel sits at the center of USC's campus, encompassing a historic home (built in 1912) connected to a wing of modern guestrooms, meeting, and dining areas. A full breakfast buffet is included with your room. During football season, standard rooms are $189, while suites range from $389 to $399. (*(803) 779-7779, innatusc.com*) ❺ **Rose Hall Bed & Breakfast:** This Queen-Anne B&B offers five guestrooms and lies in University Hill, a historic district next to the university. Guests are greeted with freshly baked cookies and, depending on the temperature, either sweet tea and lemonade, or hot mulled cider and hot chocolate. All rooms come with private baths, and all but one has its own Jacuzzi. (*(866) 771-2288, rosehallbb.com*) ❻ **The Whitney Hotel:** You're about a 20-minute walk from the university and a mile from Five Points at this all-suite hotel. The suites have separate bedrooms, living and dining areas, full kitchens, butler's tables, and balconies. The room décor is pretty traditional, but they get bonus points for providing each suite with a washer and dryer. Suites run $164–$199 during football season. (*(800) 637-4008, whitneyhotel.com*)

Where to Eat

TAILGATE SUPPLIES: ❶ **Rose-wood Market & Deli:** Whether you're a vegetarian or a meat-loving, low-carb devotee, this market has groceries for you, along with a staff to help with everything from Atkins to gluten-free diets. Rosewood offers a full selection of produce, dairy, meats, packaged items, and deli products, many of which are organic. (*(888) 203-5950, rosewoodmarket.com*) ❷ **The Gourmet Shop:** Located in the Five Points neighborhood, it's a combination grocery store, kitchen supply center, gourmet shop, and café. There's even a walk-in humidor with cigars by Onyx, Cubita, and others. If you want a gourmet tailgate party, without the toil, here's your store. They'll even supply the serving dishes. (*(803) 799-9463, thegourmetshop.net*) ❸ **The State Farmers' Market:** Ranked in the top 10 nationally for sales volume, this 50-acre extravaganza of regional farm products is owned and managed by the state of South Carolina. Better yet, it sits just across from Williams-Brice Stadium. (*(803) 734-2506, scda.state.sc.us*)

SPORTS BARS: ❹ **Icy's Sports Bistro:** They have 14 big TVs (including a couple of 52-inch HDTVs) that show just about every sporting event known to man, and food that includes surf-n-turf, fresh ravioli, or grilled seafood. Who can complain? (*$, (803) 736-5775, icyssportsbistro.com*) ❺ **State Street Pub:** It's your typical sports bar, with plenty of televised sports, pool, darts, beer, and posters on the walls. The pub's 15 TVs show every sport you can think of—except for Saturdays and Sundays. Saturdays are for college football, with up to

12 games shown at a time. On Sundays all the sets show the NFL. (*$, (803) 796-2006, statestreetpub.com*)

RESTAURANTS: ❻ **Blue Cactus Café:** Combining Southwestern and Korean cuisines may seem odd (okay, it is odd), but it works. The menu alternates between Korean and Southwest dishes, with most appetizers falling into the Korean category. The café also has more than 200 different bottles of hot sauce to sample. (*$, (803) 929-0782, bluecactuscafe.com*) ❼ **Gervais & Vine:** Sometimes you just want a little nosh and a nice glass of wine. This is the place. G&V is a great tapas and wine bar, serving a fusion of Greek, Italian, and Spanish appetizer-size treats prepared in front of you, with more than 50 wines-by-the-glass available. (*$, (803) 799-8463, gervine.com*) ❽ **Mr. Friendly's New Southern Café:** Their motto is "eat, drink, and be friendly." They do, and they are. The New-Southern cuisine menu changes frequently, but you'll find Southern favorites plus innovative seafood dishes. The menu also offers 30 microbrews and a lengthy wine list. (*$–$$, (803) 254-7828, mrfriendlys.com*)

Daytime Fun

❶ Congaree National Park: South Carolina's newest national park covers 27,000 acres of forest, wetlands, and bottomland about an hour southeast of Columbia. Here you can hike more than 25 miles of backwoods trails leading you through the nation's largest unbroken forest of old-growth hardwood trees. On Sundays, take the free ranger-guided canoe tours. (*Free, (803) 776-4396, x 0, nps.gov*) **❷ House Tours:** Columbia's historic district is well-known for its well preserved homes from the Civil War and Reconstruction eras. You can take a tour, either on your own or in a guided group, and visit any of four historic homes on your walk, including Woodrow Wilson's boyhood home and the Mann-Simons Cottage. Get your tickets in the Museum Shop on the Robert Mills House grounds at 1616 Blanding Street. (*$–$$, (803) 252-7742, historiccolumbia.org*) **❸ Riverbanks Zoo and Garden:** It's South Carolina's largest gated attraction and home to more than 2,000 animals representing more than 350 species. There are extensive collections of mammals, birds, reptiles, and fish, and several wooded trails in the 70-acre botanical garden. (*$, (803) 779-8717, riverbanks.org*) **❹ South Carolina State Museum:** The museum offers a wide range of exhibits, including art, natural and cultural history, and science and technology. In addition to permanent exhibits that feature South Carolina art, traveling exhibits keep the galleries fresh. (*$, (803) 898-4921, museum.state.sc.us*)

Nighttime Fun

❶ **The Art Bar:** It's Columbia's favorite eccentric place where all the "eeks" meet—geeks, freaks, the chic, even the occasional Greek. The bar itself is a blend of colors, mirrors, painting, and tinted light. Activities range from music and dancing to karaoke to bimonthly comedy improv performances. Oh, there's also the monthly tribal belly dance. (*$, (803) 929-0198, artbarsc.com*) ❷ **Club Ra:** As the name suggests, Club Ra is Egyptian-themed, with dance cages holding professional go-go dancers and VIP skyboxes with plasma-screen televisions. Theme nights include College S.I.N. Night and Goddess Night. The club was voted "Best Newcomer" in 2005. (*$, (803) 252-7625*) ❸ **Ghosts and Legends of Columbia:** Nightly tours of Columbia's haunted places take visitors through the State House, an Episcopal cemetery, and several other historic spots, even the USC campus. The stories of former presidents, young ladies, and Confederate soldiers may have you looking over your shoulder. Reservations are required. (*$$, (803) 765-1837, theghosts ofcarolina.com*) ❹ **Knock Knock Club:** A popular place with USC students and those just wanting to stay out late, this club attracts a pretty young crowd, but an enthusiastic one. (*$, (803) 799-1015, knockknockclub.com*)

Shopping

❶ Addams University Bookstore: If it has a Gamecock or the letters "USC" on it, it's here. This campus bookstore has a complete selection of apparel and gifts for the Carolina fan. And it is a bookstore, so you can pick up a copy of that physics textbook you've been needing. (*(803) 256-6666, bkstr.com*)

❷ Congaree Vista: Located between Assembly Street and the Congaree River, it was once a warehouse district filled with textile mills and railroad stations. Now the Vista offers more than 60 specialty shops and galleries alongside residential buildings. If you get a little hungry, there are more than 45 restaurants and bars to try. (*vistacolumbia.com*)

TENNESSEE

University of Tennessee: 25,515 students
Knoxville, TN: pop. 180,130
Neyland Stadium: seats 104,079
Colors: Orange and White
Nickname: Volunteers
Mascot: Smokey
Phone: (865) 974-6031

There's no general parking on campus. Visiting RVs can park at the Civic Coliseum and at Blackstock Street Lot behind Foundry at North World's Fair area. Cost is $25 per day, accommodating about 100 RVs, with hookups for 20. Shuttle service is provided. Tailgating starts 7 a.m. game day, runs until midnight after game. When tailgating off-campus, all local and state laws apply and are enforced. No alcohol, open fires, or tents. Visit Volunteer Village, open 3 1/2 hours before game, with interactive games, live bands, autographs, cheerleaders, and WNOX Sports-Talk's *Game Day All Day*.

Shuttle Info: Shuttles start 3 hours prior to game time. Shuttles run from Blackstone Lot at World's Fair Park, also from Coliseum, Old City, and Market Square area of downtown, $4 per person round-trip. Shuttles also run from Farragut High School, $10 per person round-trip.

Volunteers Media Partners: 990-AM WNOX, 107.7-FM WIVK

The University of Tennessee had a bumpy start. Founded in 1794 as Blount College, the school struggled for more than a decade, and in 1809 (and now known as East Tennessee College) the school's first president and only faculty member died. The school was closed.

It reopened in 1820 and in 1840 became East Tennessee University. But the Civil War dealt the university a hard blow. Students and faculty left to join both Union and Confederate forces, the school's buildings were occupied

by both armies, and shelling destroyed much of the campus. The division was devastating, but after the war the university fought back.

It became the University of Tennessee in 1879 and has grown into one of the country's prominent universities, and the Tennessee Volunteers have become one of football's most successful programs.

The Vols first hit the field in 1891, but, like the school did during its early years, the team struggled. The football program got its "official" start in 1925 with Gen. Robert Reese Neyland at the helm. Neyland coached a total of 21 years (although not consecutively) and compiled a record of 173-31-12. He's credited with building the Vols program into a major power. Under his leadership UT earned a trip to the first of its nearly 50 bowl games (that first one was a 17–0 Orange Bowl win against Oklahoma in 1938) and won national championships in 1938, 1940, 1950, and 1951 (the team won a fifth title in 1998 under Coach Phillip Fulmer). That success meant the team needed a bigger stadium, so he expanded it. Later expansions grew Neyland Stadium (it was named for the coach in 1962) into the nation's third-largest stadium. It officially seats 104,079, although a record 109,061 packed in to watch Tennessee beat Florida in 2004.

The seeds Coach Neyland planted have continued to grow. UT is the winningest team in college football since 1926 and in the top 10 of all-time winningest schools. The Vols are 1 of 4 teams to win 100 games in the 1990s (under Johnny Majors and Phillip Fulmer), and they have sent scores of players to the NFL, including Peyton

Manning, the school's all-time leading passer.

School Mascot

Tennessee (the state) is known as The Volunteer State in recognition of the spirit of support its residents gave to calls for help during the Revolutionary War, the War of 1812, the Texas Revolution, and the Mexican War. For the latter conflict Tennessee was asked to provide 2,800 volunteers to fight the war . . . 30,000 raised their hands.

> ### SMOKEY VI
> In 1991 the temperature on the field for the UCLA game hit 140 degrees, and Smokey VI suffered heat exhaustion. The mascot was listed on the team's official injury report alongside hurt players until he recovered and returned later in the season.

Tennessee (the school) first had its teams called the Volunteers, in recognition of the state's motto, in 1902 by a writer for the *Atlanta Constitution* when reporting about a game between Tennessee and Georgia Tech. The Knoxville papers began using the name in 1905, and over time it became accepted and official.

But it wasn't until 1953 that the Vols had a mascot.

That was the year the school Pep Club sponsored a mascot contest. A hound was

chosen to be the live mascot because it is a native breed to the state, and while small, its loud barking and howling represented something unique.

But exactly which hound wasn't decided until a parade of the finalists at half-time of a game. Rev. William "Bill" Brooks entered his Bluetick Coonhound, Blue Smokey. It was the ninth of nine contestants brought before the crowd, and he barked when his name was called. The students cheered, and Blue Smokey barked some more. After a few rounds of this, Tennessee had its mascot.

The mascot you see leading the team through the "T" at game time is Smokey IX.

Game-Day Traditions
Checkerboard End Zones

They are perhaps the most instantly recognizable end zones in America.

The orange-and-white checkerboard end zones debuted in 1964 when Coach Doug Dickey arrived at UT and were a part of the field until 1968, when the grass was dug up and replaced with artificial turf.

But in 1989, when the artificial turf was pulled, the tradition was reinstated along with the grass field. The colors aren't painted on; they are inlaid, contrasting colored turf.

Rocky Top

First, let me clear up one thing: "Rocky Top" is not the Tennessee fight song (that's "Down the Field").

But "Rocky Top" is the song you'll hear more than any other coming from The Pride of the Southland Band.

It was written in about 10 minutes as an upbeat diversion by songwriters Felice and Boudleaux Bryant in 1967. They were writing slower songs for Archie Campbell and Chet Atkins. It wasn't all that popular until the Tennessee band used it for one of their drills in 1972. The crowd loved it and kept asking to hear it. You don't have to ask for it anymore.

Running Through the "T"

Other schools have their team walks (UT has the Vol Walk), and other teams run onto the field through the school band's formation, but Rivals.com ranked the Vols' entrance as the sixth-best pregame tradition in college football.

The Pride of the Southland Band forms a huge, block "T" as the finishing move of its pregame performance—the "Power T," they call it—and led by Smokey the team runs through the "T" to the sideline as more than 104,000 fans cheer.

Vol Navy

George Mooney, who had been a Vol broadcaster, found fighting game-day traffic to be too stressful and time-consuming. So, in 1962, he hopped in his small boat and navigated the Tennessee River to the stadium, which sits on the river's bank. That was the first run of the Volunteer Navy.

Today the Vol Navy has grown into an armada of 200-plus boats that line up and "sterngate" in the Tennessee River before coming ashore for the game.

Tennessee Fight Song

"Down the Field"

Here's to old Tennessee
Never we'll sever
We pledge our loyalty
Forever and ever
Backing our football team
Faltering never
Cheer and fight with all of your might
For Tennessee.

Visiting Tennessee

Knoxville was the first capital of Tennessee, was Marble City in the early 1900s for all of the Tennessee Pink marble quarried here, and in the

1930s was called The Underwear Capital of the World since textile and clothing mills were the city's biggest industry. Now Knoxville is known, mostly, for being the home of the University of Tennessee. And they love their Vols here. Even the area code (865) spells VOL. Of course, the Lady Vols basketball team, under coach Pat Summitt, is also a city treasure and the big reason the Women's Basketball Hall of Fame is in Knoxville.

Where to Stay

❶ **Berry Sweet Bed & Breakfast:** There's nothing historic about this place, just a large, pleasant house on a farm in Lenoir City (about 45 minutes from Neyland Stadium), tucked into the rolling countryside. There are three guestrooms, with private baths, and UT packages are available. Rooms run $95–$135, or you can rent out the entire inn for $650 for a two-night weekend. (*(865) 765-0452, berrysweetbandb.com*) ❷ **Cumberland House Hotel:** Located across the street from campus, you can't get much closer without paying tuition. Cumber-land opened its doors in October 2006, so you get new rooms with marble sinks, cherry wood vanities, and flat-panel TVs with premium cable. Rooms run $179–$319 based on who UT's playing. (*(877) 971-4632, cumberlandhousehotel.com*) ❸ **Fox Inn Campground:** About 15 miles outside of Knoxville, there are 150 sites with full hookups, cable TV, Wi-Fi, and a dump station. Many of the sites are spaced pretty tightly with little spare room, but

ALMA MATER

On a Hallowed hill in Tennessee
Like Beacon shining bright
The stately walls of old UT.
Rise glorious to the sight.

So here's to you old Tennessee,
Our Alma Mater true
We pledge in love and harmony
Our loyalty to you.

What torches kindled at that flame
Have passed from hand to hand
What hearts cemented in that name
Bind land to stranger land.

O, ever as we strive to rise
On life's unresting stream
Dear Alma Mater, may our eyes
Be lifted to that gleam.

the facilities are well maintained. There are a good number of long-term residents here, so you may want to call ahead for big game weekends. Sites run $26–$30. (*(888) 803-9883, foxinncampground.com*) ❹ **Hotel St. Oliver:** This is a small hotel, almost more of a large B&B, with a lobby that closes at night. Many rooms have four-post or canopy beds, and each has a wet bar and refrigerator. Breakfast is served in the library during football weekends. Rooms run $80–$150, suites $175–$235. (*(865) 521-0050, angelfire.com/tn3/ stoliver/index.html*) ❺ **Maple Grove Inn:** It's one of Knoxville's oldest residences, built in 1799. There are eight guestrooms in this B&B, some of them enormous in size. The house itself is only 10 minutes from campus, but surrounded by 15 acres of landscaped property. There's an on-site restaurant available. Rooms run $125–$250. If you're okay with pink, the Holly and Pine Suites come as a pair for $220. (*(800) 645-0713, maplegroveinn.com*) ❻ **Southlake RV Park:** This is the closest RV park to Knoxville. It has 154 slots (90 are full hookups), all the basic amenities, along with cable TV, a pool, and 24-hour security. There's also a fishing dock and playground. Sites cost $22–$25; tent sites are available for $18. (*(865) 573-1837, southlakervpark.com*)

Where to Eat

TAILGATER SUPPLIES: ❶ **Three Rivers Market:** Located just a mile from downtown, this is a supermarket co-op offering everything from organic milk to dishwashing powder (also organic). Picking up your tailgate groceries here helps support Fair Trade business practices and farms that practice safe, sustainable growing methods. (*(865) 525-2069, threeriversmarket.coop*)

SPORTS BARS: ❷ **Rookies Sports Bar & Grill:** With a 100-foot-long checkerboard bar, there's room enough to grab a drink and watch the game. And you'll see the game any direction you look: there are 7 satellite TVs, 3 big-screen TVs, and 15 other monitors spread throughout the bar. There's also plenty of sports paraphernalia hung on the walls. (*(865) 691-0219*) ❸ **Rooster's:** Inside, it's a long, L-shaped room with sports décor and 22 TVs placed wherever you need them, including 2 that measure 61" and 54". The food is sports bar comfort food, along with hoagies. You can also try your luck at their

pinball machines, dart boards, or pool tables. They recently renovated and doubled their space, so don't be afraid to bring a crowd. (*$, (865) 691-3938, roosters-bar.com*)

RESTAURANTS: ❹ **The Butcher Shop:** One of several businesses created at the close of Knoxville's 1982 World's Fair, this restaurant sticks close to what it does best—steak. The Shop's steaks come in two different sizes, ranging from an 8-ounce filet to a huge 30-ounce T-bone. Diners can select a steak from the shop's cooler and slap it on one of three grills near the dining room and cook it themselves. They'll also cook it for you if you're saving your grill techniques for the parking lot. (*$$, (865) 637-0204, butchershopknoxville.com*) ❺ **Calhoun's on the River:** A Knoxville favorite, it serves smoked barbecue and its signature oysters, among a number of other dishes. If you're joining the Vol Navy for the game, you can pull up to Calhoun's on your boat and moor at the dock. Outdoor dining is available, too, on open and covered patios. (*$–$$, (865) 673-3355, calhouns.com/page.asp?id=156*) ❻ **Tomato Head:** Originally, this was going to be a French bistro, but the pizza oven changed everything. Today, it's one of Knoxville's favorite places to savor sandwiches, salads, soups, appetizers, and a wide variety of handmade pizzas. Aside from offering gourmet pizzas, the restaurant's also a venue for musical acts, poetry readings, performance art, and monthly shows highlighting local artists. (*$, (865) 637-4067, tomatohead.com*)

❼ **Sweet P's:** If you're a lazy tailgater or just forgot your charcoal, call Sweet P's. You don't go to Sweet P's; they come to you. Yep, it's a catering kitchen providing some of Knoxville's best barbecue, and they deliver racks of dry-rubbed ribs, smoked chicken, beef brisket, and pulled pork, with side items and plenty of sauce. If you need utensils or plates, they'll bring those too. This is a small, family-run operation, so call well in advance. They also deliver breakfast. (*$$, (865) 804-4843, sweetpbbq.com*)

Daytime Fun

❶ **Confederate Memorial Hall/Bleak House:** Commonly known simply as Bleak House, this 15-room mansion was used as Confederate headquarters during the siege of Knoxville in 1863, shortly before the war's end. The house is riddled with bullet holes, and one wall bears an eerie portrait of three fallen soldiers, drawn by a comrade directly on the wall itself. Guided tours take you through almost every room of this Tuscan-villa-style house, including a library

with many first-edition books and a large collection of artifacts. (*Free, (865) 522-2371, knoxvillecmh.org*) ❷ **Great Smoky Mountains National Park:** About an hour south of Knoxville is the most visited national park in the country; go there and you'll know why. The park holds more than half a million acres, with 735 miles of streams. The hiking and biking trails (all 800 miles of them) are some of the most scenic in the world. The peaks reach over 6,000 feet, giving you alpine meadows and amazing views. Visitor centers are scattered throughout, making it easy to reach countless attractions. (*Free, (865) 436-1200, nps.gov/grsm*) ❸ **Knoxville Zoo:** This 80-acre zoo includes a petting zoo, a popular bird show, and an array of animal exhibits. Popular stops are Black Bear Falls, the penguins in their natural-looking habitat, and Meerkat Lookout. If you're bringing kids, Kids Cove is a winner with a climbing wall and animal exhibits. (*$$, (865) 637-5331, knoxville-zoo.com*) ❹ **Women's Basketball Hall of Fame:** James Naismith invented basketball in 1891. Most know that. Most don't know that the next year, Senda Berenson adapted the rules for women, and women's basketball was introduced at Smith College. In the hometown of a different powerhouse women's basketball team (the Lady Vols have won six national championships and Coach Pat Summitt is the winningest Division I college basketball coach of all time), the Women's Basketball Hall of Fame opened in 1999 to celebrate and honor the women who have contributed to the sport. There are exhibits, films, interactive activities, and basketball courts (bring your game . . . and your sneakers). (*$, (865) 633-9000, wbhof.com*)

Nighttime Fun

❶ **Baker-Peters Jazz Club & Restaurant:** This restaurant/club offers an alternative to the noisy college-crowd scene. Housed in a historic mansion, with a resident ghost or two, the atmosphere's perfect for jazz. It's worth coming early to order dinner here, maybe the truffled Yukon mashed potatoes, lobster tail, and chateaubriand for two. They have a cigar menu too. (*$$, (865) 690-8110, bakerpeters jazzclub.com*) ❷ **Blue Cats:** Like a lot of live music places, you'll hear a lot of local and regional bands here. Unlike a lot of live music places, Blue Cats' music is diverse. Really diverse. One night there's a Goth ball, the next night there's hip-hop. Later in the week it's heavy-metal. Oh, did I mention the belly-dancers and the satirical, burlesque medicine show? (*$, (865) 544-4300, bluecatslive.com*) ❸ **Oodles Uncorked:** By day it's a reasonably priced

Italian restaurant; by night it transforms itself into a stylish little wine bar, with more than 50 wines available by the glass. The candlelit interior has hardwood floors and wooden chairs at the bar, with several couches along the walls. There's a small seating area outside, as well. On Friday and Saturday nights, starting around 10 p.m., you can catch live jazz, often as a free-form jam session. (*$, (865) 521-0600, oodlesuncorked.com*)   ❹ **The Strip:** Basically, any bar located on Cumberland Ave. (aka The Strip) is a popular college hangout. You'll find places to eat, drink, listen to music, dance . . . you get the idea. Some of the biggest crowds gather at **Bar Knoxville**. Inside, you'll find a large, open room, with the bar in the middle and a dance floor toward the back. TV screens are scattered throughout, while the walls are adorned with black-and-white photos and writing. Oh, and girls dance on the bar for most of the evening. (*$, (865) 566-0380, barknoxville.com*)

Shopping

❶ Bliss: In Knoxville's 150-year-old Market Square, in the heart of downtown, Bliss offers everything you need for civilized living—like colorful placemats, roomy cereal bowls, picture frames, handcrafted furniture, a selection of clocks, pillows, unique place settings, linens, and just about anything else you can think of. (*(888) 809-2424, shopinbliss.com*) **❷ Carpe Librum and McKay Used Books & CDs:** Two independent booksellers, 2 miles from one another, and two totally different experiences. Carpe Librum is a 3,000-square-foot bookstore with a sunny interior and polished wood floors. They have more than 14,000 hand-selected titles, with an excellent selection of children's and regional books. They also offer related items, stocked next to appropriate topic sections. In the science section you'll find lab equipment like beakers, flasks, and other science-related inventory. (*(865) 588-8080, carpelibrum.booksense.com*) McKay Used Books & CDs, on the other hand, is a huge warehouse-sized space holding a massive inventory of used books, CDs, DVDs, videos, audiobooks, and video games. The atmosphere is, well, there isn't any atmosphere. It's all about the inventory, and the thrill of hunting for stuff. (*(865) 588-0331, mckaybooks.com*)

❸ UT Book & Supply Stores: While lots of places around Knoxville sell some UT items, the mother lode of Vols swag is here. The main Book & Supply Store is located on the first floor of the University Center on the edge of campus, but there are six other locations around campus. As for inventory, they've got everything from logo ice scoops to OR scrub hats. In the store or online you'll spend some time browsing—eBay doesn't have this much UT stuff. (*(800) 733-8657, https://web.dii.utk.edu/utstore*) **❹ Yee-Haw Industries:** The official story is they specialize in original art-like products—from vintage-style letterpress posters to handmade, woodcut, fine art prints. But that doesn't explain items like the handcrafted Cowgirl Contortionist journal or the whacked-out calendars. Or the "Knoxville Girl" and "Tennessee Stud" T-shirts. (*(865) 522-1812, yeehawindustries.com*)

VANDERBILT

Vanderbilt University: 6,241 students
Nashville, TN: pop. 575,261
Vanderbilt Stadium: seats 39,773
Colors: Black and Gold
Nickname: Commodores
Mascot: Mr. Commodore
Phone: (615) 322-GOLD

Visiting RVs park as early as 5 p.m. Friday at Harris-Hillman School on Blakemore in Lots 106, 107, 108. RVs may stay overnight for $50 or 2 nights for $62. Cars may park on game day for $5. Cars can park at Dudley Stadium for free, or in Lots A and T for $10. Tailgating starts 7 a.m. game day and runs until midnight after game. No parking in grass or restricted areas. In Harris-Hillman lots, no amplified music or alcohol allowed. In Vandy lots no glass bottles allowed; trash and charcoal containers are available; please use them. Obey city ordinances and state laws. Visit Vandyville pregame party at south side of stadium. Vandyville has food vendors, games, and activities available, along with a 16 x 10-foot TV screen.

Shuttle Info: No shuttles. All parking within easy walking distance.

Commodores Media Partners: 650-AM and 95.5-FM WSM

Shipping and rail magnate Cornelius Vanderbilt had never been to the South, but he wanted to do something to help heal the wounds of the Civil War. His best tool: money. He had a lot of that. And in 1873 he gave $1 million to the Methodist Episcopal Church, which was trying to open Central University in Nashville but lacked funds. They had them now, and changed the name to Vanderbilt University, in his honor, of course.

Vanderbilt died in 1877 having never visited the school.

Today this school is one of the top research institutions in the country and has a nationally recognized medical center.

Vanderbilt Fight Song

"Dynamite"

Dynamite, Dynamite
When Vandy starts to fight
Down the field with blood to yield
If need be, save the shield,
If vict'rys won, when battle's done
Then Vandy's name will rise in fame,
But, win or lose, The Fates will choose,
And Vandy's game will be the same,
Dynamite, Dynamite
When Vandy Starts to Fight!

Its football team is not one of the nation's best. But it was one of its first. And it was a pretty good one in the early years.

Vanderbilt is believed to be the first school in Tennessee to field a team when it took the field in 1886. The school formed the Southern Intercollegiate Athletic Association in 1894. Vandy won the conference championship 11 times. It also won two Southern Conference championships (1922 and 1923), but it hasn't had such luck in the SEC.

The 'Dores had some good football teams in the 1940s and 1950s under Coach Jess Neely, but the team fell on hard times and would go long stretches without winning an SEC game. As the conference's smallest and only private school, it found it difficult to recruit and compete against rivals like Tennessee, Florida, and Alabama.

But in recent years the team has improved, and former quarterback Jay Cutler put himself in Vandy record books for leading the team to victory against Tennessee in Knoxville (the first time Vandy had won the match-up in more than 20 years), and later becoming a first-round NFL draft choice in 2006.

School Mascot

Cornelius Vanderbilt's nickname was "Commodore," as he made his fortune in shipping. Since Vanderbilt's fortunes created the university, Vandy's teams are the Commodores.

The term *commodore* was used by the navy in the 19th century to identify the commanding officer of a task force of ships—a rank between captain and admiral. That's why the costumed mascot, Mr. Commodore, is dressed as a naval officer from the 1880s in complete regalia.

ALMA MATER

On the city's western border
Reared against the sky
Proudly stands our Alma Mater
As the years roll by.
Forward ever be thy watchword,
Conquer and Prevail.
Hail to thee our Alma Mater,
Vanderbilt, All Hail!
Cherished by the sons and daughters,
Mem'ries sweet shall throng
Round our hearts, O Alma Mater,
As we sing our song.

Game-Day Traditions
Touchdown Foghorn

During Vandy games members of the Vanderbilt Naval ROTC Battalion can be found guarding the Touchdown Foghorn. The foghorn is from a U.S. Navy battleship and is sounded only when the Commodores score. It is a tradition that finds its roots in the nickname of the school's benefactor, "Commodore" Cornelius Vanderbilt (see School Mascot section above).

Vandyville

A relatively new tradition, Vandyville is the school's pregame tailgate party that has incorporated into it some other school traditions including the Star Walk.

One hour before kickoff, the Commodores players, dressed and ready for the game, walk from the McGugin Center to Vanderbilt Stadium through cheering fans and past the Spirit of Gold Marching Band.

Visiting Vanderbilt

Nashville is the capital of Tennessee, and the capital of country music. While the music industry is the city's most well-known, Nashville is also home to a large health care industry and, of course, tourism. It is also the only place in the world where you can find an exact replica of the Parthenon (more on that in a bit).

Where to Stay

❶ **Daisy Hill Bed & Breakfast:** The nicely appointed Tudor-style house, located on Blair Blvd., is within easy walking distance of Vanderbilt. There are three guestrooms, a library, a conservatory (sunroom), and a screened-in porch. Rooms run $110–$150. (*(800) 239-1135, daisyhillbedandbreakfast.com*) ❷ **The Hermitage Hotel:** Ritzier than the Ritz, this five-star hotel (rated by AAA) is located in the heart of downtown Nashville. Standard rooms are huge at 475 square feet and come with the amenities you'd expect. The hotel has a children's room service menu and prepared-to-order baby foods; they'll even wash and sterilize baby bottles. Pets get custom beds and their own menu. Owners can take advantage of the hotel's grooming and dog-walking service. Rooms run $200. (*(888) 888-9414, thehermitagehotel.com*) ❸ **Linden House Bed & Breakfast:** Located near the Vanderbilt campus, this turreted Victorian house is filled with antiques and unusual furnishings. Each of the three large guestrooms is painted a different, jewel-tone color, and has a private bath. Rooms run $95–$135. Children are welcome; pets are not. (*(615) 298-2701, nashville-bed-breakfast.com*) ❹ **Loews Vanderbilt Plaza:** Located directly across the street from Vanderbilt University, Loews's location is about as good as it gets. There's also a beauty salon and a clothing boutique inside, but there's not a swimming pool. On the other hand, your chances of spotting a celebrity here are better than average; a lot of them stay here when they're in town. Rooms run $170–$655. (*(615) 320-1700, loewshotels.com*) ❺ **Music Valley Drive:** Located near the Opryland Hotel and Opry Mills mall, along this street are 3 RV parks about 20 minutes from Vandy. **Two Rivers Campground** has 104 sites. While the roads are wide enough for larger motor homes to maneuver, it's an older property, so the sites aren't as wide as the roads. During football season sites run $28–$33. (*(615) 883-8559, tworiverscampground.com*) **Nashville KOA** caters to big rigs,

but there's not a lot of room for slide-outs and awnings. Prices for full hookups run $45–$57. (*(800) 562-7789, koa.com/where/tn/42148*) **Yogi Bear's Jellystone Camp Resort** has 238 sites, but they aren't paved. May–October rates run $38–$44; November–April, they're $31–$35. (*(800) 547-4480, nashville jellystone.com*)

Where to Eat

TAILGATE SUPPLIES:

❶ **Compton's Foodland:** Compton's is basically across the street from Vanderbilt. It's nothing fancy, just a small grocery store that sells the basics. But you can't beat the location . . . just walk to your tailgate party. (*(615) 327-4187*) ❷ **The Produce Place:** Only a few miles from Vanderbilt Stadium, this store is like having your own fruit and vegetable stand. You'll find a wide selection of fresh foods, including organic products and gourmet items. As the name would suggest, this is a place to get really top-quality fruits and vegetables. Most are grown locally, so you get produce at the peak of its flavor and ripeness. (*(615) 383-2664, produceplace.com*)

SPORTS BARS: ❸ **The Corner Pub Midtown:** It's a friendly, happy place serving cold beer and tasty food to neighborhood folks and Vanderbilt students—the campus is literally just around the corner. Inside, the walls are an earthy color with a platoon of flat-screen HDTVs strategically scattered about. If you're not in the mood to watch the game, you can grab a seat on the covered patio. (*$, (615) 298-9698*) ❹ **Sam's Place Sports Bar & Grill:** Just steps away from campus, this Hillsboro Village bar is a popular student hangout on game day . . . actually just about every day. Several TVs are scattered around, including on the open-air patio. Sam's has been voted "Best Sports Bar" 4 years running. (*$, (615) 383-3601*) ❺ **The Long Shot Sports Bar & Grille:** Demonbreun is hopping on the weekends, and if it's a game night, The Long Shot (formerly Two Doors Down) will be jammed with fans. This Music Row hangout has 5 HD projectors, 8 plasma screens, and 14 other HDTVs to watch whatever game you want. (*$, (615) 780-0020, myspace.com/longshotsportsbar*)

RESTAURANTS: ❻ **Blackstone's Brewery:** On West End Ave., just down the road from Vanderbilt, this is a local favorite with a better-than-average menu. Shiny brewing tanks in the front window create half a dozen beers, ranging from pale ale to dark porter. Try their sampler for an idea of just how varied beer can taste. (*$, (615) 327-9969, black*

stonebrewery.com) ❼ **Capitol Grille:** Classic, upscale American cuisine with a Southern flair sums up the Capitol Grille's take on food. Located inside the Hermitage Hotel, this restaurant is a favorite of the food magazines and also offers top-notch service. It's elegant, traditional, and formal, but a warm color scheme keeps it from feeling too stuffy or intimidating. (*$$, (888) 888-9414, thehermitagehotel.com*)

❽ **Noshville:** This is an authentic New York–style delicatessen with food you'd expect to see on New York's Broadway, rather than Nashville's. Dishes use authentic

ingredients, including some flown in from New York. Located between campus and Music Row, you're likely to find a mix of students and recording industry movers and shakers. (*$, (615) 329-NOSH, noshville.com*) ❾ **Sunset Grill:** It's home to the beautiful, the powerful, and often the famous. Diners enjoy cuisine and hip atmosphere on the patio, the main dining room, or the cozy bar. They also have a late-night menu, with many entrées from the dinner menu priced at one-half to one-third off the regular price. (*$$, (615) 386-3663, sunsetgrill.com*)

Daytime Fun

❶ **Adventure Science Center:** This children's science and learning museum is super popular, so expect to see a lot of kids with adults there. It's small enough to see everything in one day, big enough to be interesting for several hours. Dinosaurs, a planetarium, and revolving, interactive exhibits keep everything interesting. (*$, (615) 862-5160, adventuresci.com*) ❷ **Cheekwood Botanical Gardens and Museum of Art:** A former Gilded Age estate of the Cheek family (whom you can thank for creating Maxwell House Coffee), Cheekwood now serves as a center for botanical and fine arts. There are galleries within the mansion, along with collections of porcelain, silver, and other decorative arts. Don't miss the sculpture trail or greenhouses, either. There's a wildlife center, open for specific tours and programs. (*$–$$, (615) 356-8000, cheekwood.org*)

❸ **Country Music Hall of Fame and Museum:** Whether you're a fan of Hank (Sr. or Jr.), Elvis, or Kenny Chesney, the Country Music Hall of Fame and Museum celebrates the history that made Nashville Music City. (*$$, (615) 416-2001, countrymusichalloffame.com*) ❹ **Nash Trash Tours:** It's goofy, kitschy fun riding around in the Big Pink Bus with the Jugg Sisters (no, not the Judd sisters). Be prepared for gratuitous makeup advice, musical numbers, bawdy jokes, and a gossip-laced, tongue-in-cheek tour of Nashville's country music scene. You must make reservations. (*$$–$$$, (615) 226-7300, nashtrash.com*) ❺ **The Parthenon:** Built as a temporary building for the state's Centennial celebration, Nashvillians took such a liking to this exact replica of the Parthenon in Athens, Greece (as it looked pre-ruins), that it stayed. It's been renovated—including the gilding of the 42-foot statue of Athena—and it houses the city's municipal

art museum. (*$, (615) 862-8431, nashville.gov/parthenon*)

Nighttime Fun

❶ **3rd and Lindsley Bar & Grill:** Okay, so it's in an office park, but it's still a great place to eat chicken wings and listen to really good music. There's a live radio broadcast on Sundays, and the other six days of the week feature some of Nashville's best jazz and blues musicians. (*$, (615) 259-9891, 3rdandlindsley.com*) ❷ **Bar Twenty3:** This is one of Tennessee Titans quarterback Vince Young's favorite hangouts. It's been named one of the top 100 nightclubs in the country and has the crowd and celebrity sightings to back it up, along with hip styling that will make you think you're in New York, not Nashville. (*$, (615) 963-9998, bartwenty3.com*) ❸ **The Five Spot:** Located in East Nashville, just around the corner from Café Margo, this cool spot offers live, authentic New Orleans brass bands, Southern blues, and jazz. Black walls are decorated with vinyl records (which can be taken down and spun by request). (*$, (615) 650-9333, the5spot.net*) ❹ **The Grand Ole Opry:** America's longest continuously running radio show, the *Grand Ole Opry*'s been broadcasting since 1925. It's silly, often corny, and a lot of fun. Every week's lineup is different, so you never know who you might see. Top-billed country music stars often appear here, trading sets with veteran Opry performers on stage. (*$$, (615) 889-9490, opry.com*) ❺ **Lower Broad:** This stretch of Broadway in downtown Nashville has held the dreams of thousands of singers. For some, the dreams came true. This is where you'll find legendary clubs like **Tootsie's Orchid Lounge**, **Legend's Corner**, and **Robert's Western World**. You may also see a star or two stop by to sing a song. (*$, Downtown*) ❻ **The Schermerhorn Symphony Center:** Even if you're not a fan of classical music, this new, multimillion-dollar concert hall is worth visiting. The center reflects Nashville's history of neoclassical design, with its columned limestone and long colonnade. Thanks to state-of-the-art engineering technology, the center also has some of the best acoustics in the world. (*$–$$*, (615) 687-6500, *nashvillesymphony.org*)

Shopping

❶ Bookman/Bookwoman Rare and Used Books: For true book lovers, these independent book shops near Vandy offer about 150,000 pre-owned volumes, filling the shelves two-deep at times. Crowding the shelves are both well-thumbed paperbacks and more pristine hardcovers in every genre you could

want. (*(615) 383-6555, bookmanbookwoman.com*) ❷ **Fire Finch:** There's a little bit of everything here, from dazzling silk saris to lamps, flatware, pottery, cool soaps and candles, jewelry, vintage items, and even some clothing. It's fun, quirky, and tasteful. (*(615) 385-5090, firefinch.net*) ❸ **Pangaea:** Snuggle up to soft woolens from South America, enjoy Indonesian trinkets, and take in the home décor items from Mexico. Pangaea offers a combination of unique housewares and funky women's clothing. (*(615) 269-9665, pangaeanashville.com*) ❹ **Posh:** If you're ready to be fabulous, here's where to spend your dough. The store is full of up-market styles for Gen-Y men and women, with brands like Diesel, Cloth, and Miss Sixty. (*(615) 383-9840, poshonline.com*)

RECIPES

Appetizers

Soups & Salads

Sides

Main Dishes

Sweet Treats

Appetizers

TEA PUNCH

INGREDIENTS:
2 individual tea bags
1 ¼ cups boiling water
1 cup sugar
¼ cup unsweetened orange juice
⅓ cup lemon juice
1 quart ginger ale, chilled
1 orange, sliced

DIRECTIONS:
Put tea bags into boiling water. Cover and let steep 3 minutes. Pour hot tea over sugar. As soon as sugar is dissolved, add the orange and lemon juices. Strain mixture over ice in a punch bowl. Just before serving, add chilled ginger ale and orange slices.

Yields 10 servings. One serving: 5 ounces

Recipe from The Auburn Cookbook, *courtesy of the Alabama Cooperative Extension System (Alabama A&M and Auburn Universities)*

JUDY'S BLACK-EYED PEA DIP

INGREDIENTS:
1 medium onion, chopped
2 tablespoons butter
1 (15 ½-ounce) can black-eyed peas, rinsed and drained
1 (14-ounce) can artichoke hearts, chopped
2 tablespoons Parmesan cheese
½ cup sour cream
½ cup mayonnaise
1 package ranch dressing mix
4 ounces mozzarella cheese

DIRECTIONS:
Sauté onion in butter. Mix all ingredients except Mozzarella cheese together. Bake 20 minutes at 350°F. Then put Mozzarella cheese on top and heat until it melts. Serve with corn chips.

Recipe from Bully's Best Bites *cookbook, courtesy of the Junior Auxiliary of Starkville, Inc.*

PATSY'S WAR EAGLE BUFFALO CHICKEN DIP

INGREDIENTS:
2 (8-ounce) blocks of cream cheese (soften)
2 (12 ½ ounce) large cans of Tyson chicken (drained and shredded)
1 8-ounce bottle of Hidden Valley Ranch dressing (preferred brand)
Franke's REDHOT Buffalo Wing Sauce (preferred brand)

DIRECTIONS:
Mix the soften cream cheese and the ranch dressing; add the shredded chicken; add wing sauce to taste (approx ⅓ of the bottle). Option: cover with 2 cups shredded sharp cheddar cheese and bake at 350°F until cheese is melted. Serve with SCOOPS Frito chips. (You'll need the family-sized bag.)

Patsy M. Carter, Auburn University

SPICY TWO-THREE GARDEN APPETIZER

INGREDIENTS:
16 ounces fat-free cream cheese, softened
1 cup nonfat sour cream
2 tablespoons taco seasoning mix
1 cup mild or hot taco sauce
1 cup (4 ounces) shredded reduced-fat cheddar cheese
½ cup chopped green onions
½ cup chopped green bell pepper
½ cup chopped tomato

DIRECTIONS:
Beat the cream cheese, sour cream, and taco seasoning mix in a medium mixing bowl until smooth. Spread evenly on a 12- to 14-inch glass serving platter. Drizzle with the taco sauce. Sprinke with the cheese, green onions, bell pepper, and tomato. Chill covered until ready to serve. Serve with baked tortilla chips or snack crackers.

Yields 10 servings

Recipe from Pride of Kentucky *cookbook, courtesy University of Kentucky Cooperative Extension Service and Kentucky Department of Agriculture*

MUSHROOMS STUFFED WITH SWEET SAUSAGE

INGREDIENTS:

24 large fresh mushrooms

2 tablespoons oil

½ cup chopped onion

1 tablespoon minced garlic

½ pound Bryan light pampered pork sausage

½ teaspoon ground cinnamon

¼ teaspoon ground nutmeg

1 teaspoon toasted fennel seed, ground

1 tablespoon grated orange zest

¼ cup dried bread crumbs

Salt and freshly ground pepper to taste

1 cup chicken stock

DIRECTIONS:

Remove the stems from the mushrooms and chop them; reserve caps. Heat oil in large sauté pan. Add chopped onion and cook until soft, about 5 minutes. Add chopped mushroom stems and cook over high heat until mushrooms start to become dry, about 5 minutes. Stir in garlic and cook for 1 minute. Transfer to a bowl and set the mixture aside. Cook sausage, breaking it up with a fork, until it is no longer pink, about 5 minutes. Stir in next 4 ingredients. Add cooked mushroom and onion mixture and bread crumbs; mix well. Season with salt and pepper and adjust the rest of the spices. Preheat oven to 350°F. Stuff the pork mixture into the mushroom caps. Place mushrooms in a baking pan and drizzle the stock around them. Bake until cooked through, about 20 to 25 minutes. Serve warm.

Recipe from Bully's Best Bites *cookbook, courtesy of the Junior Auxiliary of Starkville, Inc.*

EASY VEGETABLE DIP

INGREDIENTS:
2 cups 1% lowfat cottage cheese
½ cup finely chopped celery
¼ cup finely grated carrots
¼ cup chopped chives
2 tablespoons reduced-calorie, cholesterol-free mayonnaise
2 tablespoons nonfat plain yogurt
3 tablespoons mustard-flavored mayonnaise
3 tablespoons lemon juice

DIRECTIONS:
Beat cottage cheese with an electric beater until it is smooth and fluffy. Add vegetables and mix well. Add remaining ingredients and stir until well blended. Cover and chill at least 1 hour.

Recipe from The Auburn Cookbook, *courtesy of the Alabama Cooperative Extension System (Alabama A&M and Auburn Universities)*

SPICY PECANS

INGREDIENTS:
2 pounds pecan halves
1 stick butter
Onion salt
Freshly ground pepper

DIRECTIONS:
Heat oven to 275° F. Melt butter in large iron skillet. Add pecans and toss to coat well. Sprinkle generously with onion salt and freshly ground pepper. Continue to toss gently for a few minutes. Put in oven and bake for about 20 minutes, or until pecans are crisp. Delicious served hot or at room temperature.

Recipe from Winning Seasons *cookbook, courtesy of the Junior League of Tuscaloosa, Inc.*

GREEN SOY NUTS

INGREDIENTS:
1 pound raw, unshelled green soybeans

DIRECTIONS:
Cook unshelled green soybeans in boiling salted water for 30 minutes or until tender. Shell and eat like boiled peanuts.

Recipe from The Auburn Cookbook, *Alabama Cooperative Extension System (Alabama A&M and Auburn Universities), revised 1996. Used by permission. All rights reserved.*

CAMPBELLSVILLE CHEESE BALL

INGREDIENTS:
16 ounces cream cheese, softened
2 ½ cups (10 ounces) shredded cheddar cheese, at room temperature
1 tablespoon chopped pimento
1 tablespoon chopped onion
1 tablespoon chopped bell pepper
2 teaspoons Worcestershire sauce
1 teaspoon lemon juice
1 cup finely chopped pecans

DIRECTIONS:
Combine the cream cheese and cheddar cheese in a bowl and mix well. Add the pimento, onion, bell pepper, Worcestershire sauce, and lemon juice and mix well. Chill covered in the refrigerator. Shape into one or two balls. Roll in the chopped pecans.

Yields 32 servings

Recipe from Pride of Kentucky *cookbook, courtesy University of Kentucky Cooperative Extension Service and Kentucky Department of Agriculture*

WATERMELON RIND PICKLES

INGREDIENTS:
2 pounds prepared watermelon rind
Lime water made from 1 quart water and 1 tablespoon builder's lime
1 quart clear, distilled vinegar, divided
1 cup water
5 cups sugar (2 ½ pounds)
1 tablespoon whole allspice
1 tablespoon whole cloves
6 small pieces stick cinnamon

DIRECTIONS:
Trim outer green skin and pink portions from watermelon rind. Cut in desired size and soak for 2–3 hours in lime water. Drain and rinse rind. Cover it with fresh cold water and boil for 1 hour, or until tender. Drain the watermelon. Cover with weak vinegar solution (1 cup vinegar to 2 cups water), and allow to stand overnight. Discard the liquid the next morning and make a syrup of 3 cups remaining vinegar, 1 cup water, sugar, and spices. Heat syrup to simmering point. Remove from heat; cover and steep for 1 hour to extract flavor of spices. Add the drained watermelon to syrup and cook gently for 2 hours or until syrup is fairly thick. Pack in pint standard canning jars. Adjust lids and process in boiling water bath canner (212°F) for 15 minutes. Note: Must be cooked in enamel or stainless steel or pickles will turn dark!

Recipe from Winning Seasons *cookbook, courtesy of the Junior League of Tuscaloosa, Inc*

CHEESE STRAWS

INGREDIENTS:
½ cup corn-oil margarine
2 cups grated sharp cheddar cheese
1 ½ cups all-purpose flour
½ teaspoon salt (optional)
¾ teaspoon baking powder
½ teaspoon dry mustard
⅛ teaspoon cayenne pepper, or to taste

DIRECTIONS:
Beat margarine until soft and smooth. Gradually add grated cheese, beating after each addition. Continue to beat until mixture is light and creamy. Measure flour into a medium-size bowl. Combine salt, baking powder, mustard, and cayenne and add to flour. Stir to blend. Gradually add flour mixture to cheese mixture, mixing well after each addition. If you have a cookie press, follow manufacturer's directions for shaping cheese straws. If you do not have a cookie press, wrap dough and chill thoroughly. Then place on a lightly floured surface. Roll dough to ⅛ to ¼ inch thick. Cut into ½ x 1 ½-inch strips. Place strips on an ungreased baking sheet. Bake at 350°F for 10 to 12 minutes. Remove from pan and cool on a wire rack covered with absorbent paper. Store the same as for crisp cookies.

Recipe from The Auburn Cookbook, *courtesy of the Alabama Cooperative Extension System (Alabama A&M and Auburn Universities)*

SUMMER FRUIT SALAD

INGREDIENTS:
1 cantaloupe, peeled and cut into ¾-inch cubes
1 (20-ounce) can pineapple chunks in juice, undrained
1 unpeeled apple, cubed
2 peaches, peeled and cut into wedges
1 cup strawberries, halved
1 cup blueberries
1 cup grapes, halved
1 (6-ounce) can frozen orange juice concentrate, thawed and undiluted
2 bananas, peeled and cut in ½-inch slices

DIRECTIONS:
Layer fruits in large bowl in order given, except bananas. Pour orange juice concentrate over. Cover and chill for 6–8 hours. Add bananas an hour before serving.

Yields 10 to 12 servings

Recipe from Winning Seasons *cookbook, courtesy of the Junior League of Tuscaloosa, Inc.*

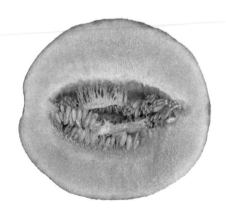

VIDALIA ONION SOUP

INGREDIENTS:
4 to 5 large Vidalia or sweet onions, chopped
3 tablespoons butter or margarine
¼ teaspoon pepper
1 tablespoon all-purpose flour
4 cups beef broth
1 ½ cups water
1 bay leaf
8 slices French bread, toasted
½ cup shredded Swiss cheese

DIRECTIONS:
In Dutch oven or soup kettle, sauté the onion in butter until lightly browned. Sprinkle with pepper and flour. Cook and stir for 1 minute. Add broth, water, and bay leaf; simmer for 30 to 40 minutes, stirring occasionally. Discard bay leaf. Ladle into oven-proof soup bowls (or 1 large casserole), top with bread and cheese. Bake at 400°F for 10 minutes or until cheese is golden brown.

Yields 2 quarts or 8 servings

Recipe from Bully's Best Bites *cookbook, courtesy of the Junior Auxiliary of Starkville, Inc.*

ALMOND BIBB SALAD

INGREDIENTS:
1 head Bibb lettuce or romaine, torn
¼ head iceberg lettuce, torn
½ cup thinly sliced celery
2 green onions, thinly sliced
¼ cup soybean oil
2 tablespoons sugar, or an equivalent amount of sugar substitute
2 tablespoons wine vinegar
1 tablespoon snipped fresh parsley
½ teaspoon salt
⅛ teaspoon red pepper sauce
1 (11-ounce) can mandarin oranges, drained
½ cup sliced almonds, toasted
1 purple onion, sliced (optional)

DIRECTIONS:
Place the Bibb lettuce, iceberg lettuce, celery, and green onions in a large
sealable plastic bag and seal the bag. Store in the refrigerator until ready
to serve. Mix the soybean oil, sugar, wine vinegar, parsley, salt, and red
pepper sauce in a jar with a tight-fitting lid. Chill, covered, until ready to
serve. To serve, pour the dressing over the lettuce mixture and seal the
bag. Shake the bag well to coat. Arrange the lettuce mixture on individual
salad plates. Top with the mandarin oranges, almonds, and purple onion
rings.

Yields 6 servings

Recipe from Pride of Kentucky *cookbook, courtesy University of Kentucky
Cooperative Extension Service and Kentucky Department of Agriculture*

CAROL'S CHEDDAR CHEESE CHOWDER

INGREDIENTS:
2 cups boiling water
2 cups potatoes, cubed
½ cup carrots, sliced
½ cup celery, sliced
½ cup onion, chopped
1 ½ teaspoons salt
¼ teaspoon white pepper
¼ cup margarine
¼ cup flour
2 cups milk
2 cups (8-ounces) sharp cheddar cheese, shredded
1 cup cooked ham, chopped or 8 slices crispy cooked bacon, crumbled

DIRECTIONS:
Add water to potatoes, carrots, celery, onion, salt, and pepper. Cover; simmer 10 minutes. Do not drain. Make white sauce by mixing margarine, flour, and milk together and cooking over low heat. Pour some of the water from vegetables into the sauce to keep it from curdling. Add sauce to vegetables. Add cheese; stir until melted. Add ham or bacon. Heat; do not boil.

Yields 4 servings

Recipe from Bully's Best Bites *cookbook, courtesy of the Junior Auxiliary of Starkville, Inc.*

SPICY RED POTATO SALAD

INGREDIENTS:
15 red potatoes
1 ½ cups mayonnaise
5 medium hard-cooked eggs, chopped
2 teaspoons garlic powder
1 cup chopped onions
½ cup chopped celery
½ cup chopped green bell pepper
½ teaspoon salt
½ teaspoon black pepper
¼ teaspoon red bell pepper flakes

DIRECTIONS:
Scrub the potatoes. Place in a saucepan and cover with water. Cook over medium-high heat for 20 minutes or until soft. Drain and rinse under cold water. Drain again and blot with paper towels until room temperature. Place the potatoes in a bowl and chop coarsely with a knife. Add the mayonnaise, hard-cooked eggs, mayonnaise, garlic powder, onions, celery, bell pepper, salt, black pepper, and red pepper flakes. Chill covered for 1 hour before serving.

Yields 12 servings

Recipe from Pride of Kentucky *cookbook, courtesy University of Kentucky Cooperative Extension Service and Kentucky Department of Agriculture*

SQUASH A LA BAMA

INGREDIENTS:
1 pound squash
½ stick oleo
1 egg
½ cup mayonnaise
2 tablespoons onion, chopped
2 tablespoons green pepper, chopped
1 cup grated cheese
½ package cracker or bread crumbs
Chopped pimento for color

DIRECTIONS:
Clean, slice, and boil squash until tender. Drain squash and mix with other ingredients. Bake in buttered casserole dish at 350°F for 30-35 minutes.

Yields 6 servings

Recipe from Winning Seasons *cookbook, courtesy of the Junior League of Tuscaloosa, Inc.*

CRAB STUFFED POTATOES

INGREDIENTS:
4 large baking potatoes
1 stick butter
1 (8-ounce) carton sour cream
2 to 3 teaspoons milk
Salt and pepper to taste
1 (6 ½-ounce) can crabmeat, drained

DIRECTIONS:
Bake potatoes. Cut in half, scoop out center while still hot. Blend it together with remaining ingredients and restuff into potato shells. Reheat at 350°F until hot. May be made ahead and refrigerated overnight.

Recipe from Bully's Best Bites *cookbook, courtesy of the Junior Auxiliary of Starkville, Inc.*

BOURBON BARBECUED BEANS

INGREDIENTS:

4 slices bacon, chopped into ½-inch pieces
1 cup chopped yellow onion
1 tablespoon minced garlic
½ cup ketchup
¼ cup dark molasses
¼ cup prepared mustard
⅓ cup bourbon
2 tablespoons brown sugar
2 tablespoons Worcestershire sauce
⅜ teaspoon hot sauce
2 (28-ounce) cans baked beans
Salt and pepper to taste

DIRECTIONS:

Prepare smoking packets for the grill by soaking mesquite or hickory chips in water to cover for 30 minutes; drain. Wrap the chips loosely in 4x4-inch pieces of foil and pierce several holes in the top to allow the smoke to escape. Place the packets in the bottom of the grill before preheating. Cook the bacon in a large sauté pan over medium heat for 10 minutes or until crisp, stirring occasionally. Add the onion and garlic. Sauté for 5 minutes or until soft. Add the ketchup, molasses, mustard, bourbon, brown sugar, Worcestershire sauce, and hot sauce and mix well. Bring to a boil and reduce the heat. Simmer for 5 minutes. Rinse the beans and drain. Place in a 2-quart heatproof baking dish. Add the sauce and mix well. Place on a rack over the prepared grill. Grill for 1 ½ hours over indirect medium heat. Season with salt and pepper to taste.

Yields 15 servings

Recipe from Pride of Kentucky *cookbook, courtesy University of Kentucky Cooperative Extension Service and Kentucky Department of Agriculture*

CORN PUDDING

INGREDIENTS:
8 tablespoons melted butter
2 tablespoons self-rising flour
1 teaspoon salt
2 tablespoons sugar
4 beaten eggs
2 cups fresh corn or 1 (10-ounce) package Tennessee brand
   frozen cream corn
1 cup milk

DIRECTIONS:
Preheat oven to 325°F. Blend butter, flour, salt, and sugar. Add beaten
eggs. Stir in corn and then milk. Pour in casserole and bake for 45 minutes
at 325°F.

Yields 8 servings

Recipe from Winning Seasons *cookbook, courtesy of the Junior League of
Tuscaloosa, Inc.*

Main Dishes

AU-SOME BURGERS

INGREDIENTS:
1 pound ground beef
1 pound ground chuck
2 green onions, diced
¾ cup sun-dried tomatoes in oil, drained and finely chopped
6 ounce crumbled herbed feta cheese
1 cup fresh baby spinach, finely chopped
2 tablespoons fresh dill, minced
2 teaspoons kosher salt
1 teaspoon fresh ground pepper
1 teaspoon garlic powder
1 tablespoon Worcestershire

DIRECTIONS:
Combine all ingredients and mix well. Cover and let the mixture sit for 30 minutes in refrigerator. Form into 8 patties. Cook on a charcoal grill. For added flavor, add hickory chips to coals prior to cooking. Do not press burgers; this will keep them juicy.

Yields 8 burgers

Scott Davis, Network Engineer, Auburn University College of Architecture, Design, and Construction

BARBECUED CATFISH

INGREDIENTS:
4 tablespoons reduced-calorie margarine
½ cup chicken broth
¼ cup fresh lemon juice
½ cup water
1 tablespoon Worcestershire sauce
¼ teaspoon white pepper
1 teaspoon dry mustard
1 tablespoon brown sugar
6 catfish fillets, about 4 ounces each
Butter-flavor vegetable cooking spray

DIRECTIONS:
To make barbecue sauce, combine the margarine, broth, lemon juice, water, Worcestershire sauce, pepper, mustard, and brown sugar in a saucepan. Heat until margarine melts. Place fillets in a baking dish and pour the sauce over them. Cover and refrigerate for 1 or 2 hours. Coat the rack of a cold broiler pan with cooking spray. Place fillets on rack and brush with barbecue sauce. Broil 5 to 6 inches from heat for 5 to 6 minutes. Baste often with the sauce. Carefully turn and brush the other side. Broil for 6 to 7 minutes longer, basting often. Bake until fish flakes easily with a fork. Serve hot.

Yields 6 servings

Recipe from The Auburn Cookbook, *courtesy of the Alabama Cooperative Extension System (Alabama A&M and Auburn Universities)*

FRIED TURKEY

INGREDIENTS:
1 (9- to 13-pound) turkey
¼ cup creole seasoning
3 tablespoons black pepper, coarsely ground
3 tablespoons salt
3 tablespoons cayenne pepper
2 tablespoons garlic powder
1 tablespoon Greek seasoning
4 to 6 gallons peanut oil

DIRECTIONS:
Mix seasonings together. Rub turkey inside and outside with seasonings, working seasoning under skin directly on the meat. Refrigerate seasoned turkey 8 to 12 hours before frying. To fry turkey, fill a 4- to 6-gallon cast iron wash pot with peanut oil. Place on butane burner and preheat to 350°F. Place prepared turkey in peanut oil and cook 4 minutes per pound or until turkey floats in oil and bubbling ceases. Best served when hot.

Yields 6 to 8 servings

Recipe from Bully's Best Bites *cookbook, courtesy of the Junior Auxiliary of Starkville, Inc.*

GRILLED PORK TENDERLOIN

INGREDIENTS:
½ cup peanut oil
⅓ cup soy sauce
¼ cup red wine vinegar
3 tablespoons lemon juice
2 tablespoons Worcestershire sauce
1 garlic clove, crushed
1 tablespoon chopped fresh parsley
1 tablespoon dry mustard
1 ½ teaspoons pepper
2 (¾ to 1-pound) pork tenderloins

DIRECTIONS:
Combine the peanut oil, soy sauce, wine vinegar, lemon juice,
Worcestershire sauce, garlic, parsley, dry mustard, and pepper in a heavy-
duty sealable plastic bag and shake to mix well. Add the pork and turn to
coat. Seal the bag. Marinate in the refrigerator for 4 hours or longer,
turning occasionally. Drain the pork, discarding the marinade. Place the
pork on a grill rack. Grill, covered, over medium coals (300 to 400°F) until
a meat thermometer inserted into the thickest portion registers 160°F.

Yields 6 servings

Recipe from Pride of Kentucky *cookbook, courtesy University of Kentucky
Cooperative Extension Service and Kentucky Department of Agriculture*

BARBECUED PORK ON BUNS

INGREDIENTS:
2 cups chopped cooked pork
¼ cup chopped green bell pepper
2 tablespoons pork drippings
½ cup ketchup
2 teaspoons prepared mustard
2 tablespoons water
2 tablespoons brown sugar
1 tablespoon instant minced onion
1 tablespoon Worcestershire sauce
½ teaspoon salt
4 hamburger buns, split

DIRECTIONS:
Lightly brown the pork and bell pepper in the pork drippings in the skillet; drain. Add the ketchup, mustard, water, brown sugar, onions, Worcestershire sauce, and salt and mix well. Cook over low heat for 20 to 25 minutes, stirring occasionally. Spoon onto the bottom halves of the buns. Top with the remaining halves.

Yields 4 servings

Recipe from Pride of Kentucky *cookbook, courtesy University of Kentucky Cooperative Extension Service and Kentucky Department of Agriculture*

GRILLED CATFISH

INGREDIENTS:
4 catfish fillets
Vinegar
Cajun seasoning
Greek seasoning
Seasoned salt
Seasoned pepper

DIRECTIONS:
With a sharp knife make slits in catfish fillets and sprinkle with vinegar.
Then sprinkle with the seasonings to taste and allow to stand 20 to 30
minutes. Turn catfish, and repeat seasoning process. Grill over medium
coals 8 to 10 minutes per side. A wire fish basket is preferable.

Yields 4 servings

Recipe from Bully's Best Bites *cookbook, courtesy of the Junior Auxiliary of
Starkville, Inc.*

METCALFE MEATBALLS

INGREDIENTS:
3 pounds ground round
1 (12-ounce) can evaporated milk
1 cup chopped onion
½ teaspoon garlic powder
2 teaspoons salt
½ teaspoon pepper
2 eggs, lightly beaten
2 tablespoons chili powder
2 cups rolled oats
2 cups packed brown sugar
4 cups ketchup
1 cup chopped onion
1 teaspoon garlic powder

DIRECTIONS:
Combine the ground round, evaporated milk, onions, garlic powder, salt, pepper, eggs, chili powder, and oats in a large bowl and mix well. Shape into golf ball-size balls. Place in a 9x13-inch baking dish sprayed with nonstick cooking spray. Mix the ketchup, brown sugar, onion, and garlic powder in a bowl. Pour over the meatballs. Cover with foil. Bake at 350°F for 1 hour or until the meatballs are cooked through.

Yields 20 servings

Recipe from Pride of Kentucky *cookbook, courtesy University of Kentucky Cooperative Extension Service and Kentucky Department of Agriculture*

PUNCH AND JUDY CHILI

INGREDIENTS:

3 tablespoons butter or olive oil

1 large onion, minced

2 cloves garlic, minced

¾ pound chopped beef (or ground)

½ pound chopped pork (approximately 2 pork chops)

2 cups water

1 ⅓ cups canned tomatoes

1 green pepper, minced

½ teaspoon celery seed

¼ teaspoon cayenne

1 teaspoon cumin seed, crushed

1 small bay leaf

2 tablespoons chili powder

½ teaspoon basil

1 ⅓ teaspoons salt

1 (15-ounce) can kidney beans

DIRECTIONS:

Heat the butter in a skillet. Add the onions and garlic and sauté until golden brown. Add the meat and brown. Transfer the meat mixture to a large saucepan and add water, tomatoes, pepper, celery seed, cayenne, cumin, bay leaf, chili powder, basil, and salt. Bring to a boil, then reduce the heat and simmer, uncovered, until the sauce is as thick as desired or about 3 hours. If desired, add one can of kidney beans just before serving. Freezes well; freeze prior to adding beans.

Yields 4 servings

Recipe from Winning Seasons *cookbook, courtesy of the Junior League of Tuscaloosa, Inc.*

HONEY-GINGERED PORK TENDERLOIN

INGREDIENTS:
2 ¾-pound pork tenderloins
¼ cup honey
¼ cup soy sauce
2 tablespoons brown sugar
1 tablespoon plus 1 teaspoon minced fresh ginger
1 tablespoon minced garlic
1 tablespoon catsup
¼ teaspoon onion powder
¼ teaspoon ground red pepper
¼ teaspoon ground cinnamon
Fresh parsley, optional

DIRECTIONS:
Place tenderloins in an 11x7x1½-baking dish. Combine honey and next 8 ingredients, stirring well; pour over tenderloins. Cover and marinate in refrigerator 8 hours, turning occasionally. Remove tenderloins from marinade, reserving marinade. Grill tenderloins over medium-hot coals 25 to 35 minutes, turning often and basting with reserved marinade. To serve, slice tenderloins thinly and arrange on a serving platter. Garnish with fresh parsley, if desired.

Yields 6 servings

Recipe from Bully's Best Bites *cookbook, courtesy of the Junior Auxiliary of Starkville, Inc.*

HONEY MUSTARD BARBECUE BEEFWICHES

INGREDIENTS:
½ recipe Two-Way Shredded Beef (page 198)
1 cup honey mustard barbecue sauce
4 hamburger buns or Kaiser rolls, split
Chopped green bell pepper (optional)
Chopped sweet onion (optional)

DIRECTIONS:
Combine the Two-Way Shredded Beef and barbecue sauce in a 1 ½-quart microwave-safe dish. Microwave, covered, on high for 5 to 6 minutes or until heated through, stirring once. Spread equal amounts of the beef mixture on the bottom halves of the buns. Sprinkle with chopped green bell pepper and chopped sweet onion. Top with the remaining halves of the buns.

Yields 4 servings

Recipe from Pride of Kentucky *cookbook, courtesy University of Kentucky Cooperative Extension Service and Kentucky Department of Agriculture*

PORK-A-BOBS

INGREDIENTS:
4 to 6 thick pork chops
¼ cup soy sauce
¼ cup lemon juice
¼ cup salad oil
¼ cup parsley, chopped
¼ teaspoon salt
¼ teaspoon pepper
1 (15-ounce) can mandarin oranges
1 (20-ounce) can pineapple chunks
3 bell peppers
Mushrooms

DIRECTIONS:
Cube pork chops. Combine soy sauce, lemon juice, salad oil, parsley, salt, and pepper to make a marinade. Place cubed chops in marinade 2 hours. Partially cook in microwave at medium-level power about 5 minutes, turn, and then cook 5 minutes more. Cut up bell pepper. On skewers alternate meat, oranges, pineapple, bell peppers, and mushrooms. Grill.

Yields 4 to 6 servings

Recipe from Bully's Best Bites *cookbook, courtesy of the Junior Auxiliary of Starkville, Inc.*

TWO-WAY SHREDDED BEEF

INGREDIENTS:
1 medium onion, cut into quarters
3 garlic cloves
1 (3- to 3 ¼-pound) boneless beef chuck shoulder or bottom round roast,
   cut into 4 pieces
1 teaspoon salt
½ teaspoon pepper
¾ cup water

DIRECTIONS:
Place the onion, garlic, and beef in a slow cooker. Sprinkle with the salt
and pepper. Add the water. Cook, covered, on low for 9 to 9 ½ hours or
until the beef is tender. Remove the beef from the cooking liquid and
discarding the solids. Skim the top of the reserved liquid. Trim the beef.
Shred the beef using 2 forks. Divide the shredded beef into 2 equal
portions. Add ¼ cup of the reserved cooking liquid to each portion. Use to
prepare Tex-Mex Beef Wraps or Honey Mustard Barbecue Beefwiches.
(You may store, covered, in the refrigerator for up to 4 days.)

Yields 8 servings

Recipe from Pride of Kentucky *cookbook, courtesy University of Kentucky
Cooperative Extension Service and Kentucky Department of Agriculture*

BLACKENED CHICKEN

INGREDIENTS:
4 to 6 chicken breasts, skinned
½ to ¾ of 10-ounce bottle soy sauce

DIRECTIONS:
Marinate chicken in soy sauce, breast side down overnight or at least 2 hours. Bake in 350°F oven for 30 minutes. Cook on grill for an additional 30 minutes or until done.

Yields 4 to 6 servings

Recipe from Bully's Best Bites *cookbook, courtesy of the Junior Auxiliary of Starkville, Inc.*

TEX-MEX BEEF WRAPS

INGREDIENTS:
½ cup frozen whole kernel corn
1 small tomato, chopped
1 tablespoon chopped cilantro
1 (16-ounce) jar thick-and-chunky salsa
½ recipe Two-Way Shredded Beef (page 198)
2 tablespoons chopped cilantro
4 (10-inch) flour tortillas, warmed

DIRECTIONS:
Combine the corn, tomato, 1 tablespoon cilantro, and 2 tablespoons of the prepared salsa in a bowl. Chill, covered, in the refrigerator until ready to serve. Combine the Two-Way Shredded Beef, remaining prepared salsa, and 2 tablespoons cilantro in a 1 ½-quart microwave-safe dish. Microwave, covered, on high for 7 to 8 minutes or until heated through, stirring once. Spoon ½ of the beef mixture evenly over each tortilla, leaving a 1 ½-inch border around the edge. Top each with ¼ cup of the corn mixture. Fold the right and left edges of the tortilla over the filling. Fold the bottom edge up and roll up. Garnish with additional chopped cilantro and serve immediately.

Yields 4 servings

Recipe from Pride of Kentucky *cookbook, courtesy University of Kentucky Cooperative Extension Service and Kentucky Department of Agriculture*

SALMON STUFFED WITH SHRIMP DRESSING

INGREDIENTS:
3 tablespoons olive oil
2 stalks celery, chopped
1 bunch green onions, chopped
1 teaspoon garlic
3 tablespoons parsley, minced
½ pound shrimp, chopped
6 ounces crabmeat
4 to 6 ounces Italian bread crumbs
1 4- to 6-pound whole salmon
1 lemon, thinly sliced

DIRECTIONS:
Sauté celery, onions, and garlic in oil until tender. Add parsley and shrimp.
Cook until shrimp turns pink. Remove from heat and let cool. Add
crabmeat and bread crumbs. Stuff salmon with dressing and secure with
skewers, large toothpicks, or string. Top with lemon slices. Cook in smoker
for 3 hours.

Yields 10 to 12 servings

Recipe from Bully's Best Bites *cookbook, courtesy of the Junior Auxiliary of Starkville, Inc.*

SLOW COOKER MOUNT ST. JOSEPH BURGOO

INGREDIENTS:
8 ounces cooked boneless skinless chicken, chopped
4 ounces cooked beef roast, chopped
1 cooked boneless pork chop, chopped
4 potatoes, cut into cubes
¼ cup lima beans, cooked
¼ cup navy beans, cooked
3 ¼ cups chopped tomatoes
1 ½ cups shredded cabbage
¼ cup whole kernel corn
⅓ cup Worcestershire sauce
2 tablespoons vinegar
1 teaspoon sugar
Salt and pepper to taste
3 cups water

DIRECTIONS:
Combine the chicken, beef, pork, potatoes, lima beans, navy beans, tomatoes, cabbage, corn, Worcestershire sauce, vinegar, sugar, salt, pepper, and water in a slow cooker and mix well. Cook on low for 8 hours. (You may substitute barbecued pork or mutton for one of the meats.)

Yields 15 servings

Recipe from Pride of Kentucky *cookbook, courtesy University of Kentucky Cooperative Extension Service and Kentucky Department of Agriculture*

EDEN SHALE SLOPPY JOES

INGREDIENTS:

1 tablespoon vegetable oil
  or shortening

½ cup minced onion

½ cup chopped celery

½ cup chopped green bell pepper

½ cup shredded carrots

1 ¼ pounds ground round

½ cup ketchup

½ cup water

1 teaspoon chili powder

½ teaspoon salt

¼ teaspoon pepper

⅛ teaspoon hot pepper sauce

8 whole wheat sandwich buns, split

DIRECTIONS:

Heat the oil in a large skillet over medium heat. Add the onion, celery, bell
pepper, and carrots. Sauté until tender. Add the ground round. Cook until
brown and crumbly, stirring constantly; drain. Stir in the ketchup, water,
chili powder, salt, pepper, and hot pepper sauce. Simmer, uncovered, over
low heat for 15 minutes or until thickened. Spoon onto the bottom halves
of the buns. Top with the remaining halves of the buns. (This is a quick
and easy meal that lets you camouflage vegetables for picky eaters.)

Yields 8 servings

Recipe from Pride of Kentucky *cookbook, courtesy University of Kentucky
Cooperative Extension Service and Kentucky Department of Agriculture*

FRIED DIXIE CHICKEN

INGREDIENTS:
1 (2- to 3-pound) broiler-fryer chicken, cut up
Salt and pepper
2 cups all-purpose flour
1 teaspoon red pepper
1 egg, slightly beaten
½ cup milk
Hot oil

DIRECTIONS:
Season chicken with salt and pepper. Combine flour and red pepper; set aside. Combine egg and milk; dip chicken in egg mixture; then dredge in flour mixture, coating well. Heat 1 inch of oil in a skillet; place chicken in skillet. Cover and cook over medium heat about 30 minutes or until golden brown, turning occasionally. Drain on paper towels. Serve with Cream Gravy.

Yields 4 servings

CREAM GRAVY INGREDIENTS:
4 tablespoons drippings
4 tablespoons all-purpose flour
2 ½ to 3 cups hot milk
Salt and pepper

DIRECTIONS:
Pour off all except 4 tablespoons drippings in which chicken was fried; place skillet over medium heat; add flour and stir until browned. Gradually add hot milk. Cook, stirring constantly, until thickened. Add salt and pepper to taste. Serve hot.

Yields about 2 cups

Both recipes from Winning Seasons *cookbook, courtesy of the Junior League of Tuscaloosa, Inc.*

BARBECUED CHICKEN

MARINADE INGREDIENTS:
1 (3-pound) fryer, quartered
1 large garlic clove, crushed
1 teaspoon salt
½ teaspoon freshly ground pepper
1 tablespoon oil
3 tablespoons lemon juice

BARBECUE SAUCE INGREDIENTS:
¼ cup cider vinegar
2 ¼ cups water
¾ cup sugar
1 stick butter or margarine
⅓ cup yellow mustard
2 onions, coarsely chopped
½ teaspoon each salt and pepper
½ cup Worcestershire
2 ½ cups catsup
6 to 8 tablespoons lemon juice
Cayenne pepper to taste

MARINADE DIRECTIONS:
Put marinade ingredients into a heavy Ziploc bag. Shake to coat well. Refrigerate for 24 hours if possible, turning the bag several times. When coals are ready, place chicken on the grill, skin side up basting with the marinade. Cook until well browned before turning. If baking in the oven, bake at 400°F, skin side down first. About 20 minutes before chicken is done, begin using your favorite bottle barbeque sauce or the homemade version above.

BARBECUE SAUCE DIRECTIONS:

Combine vinegar, water, sugar, butter, mustard, onions, salt, and pepper together and bring to a boil. Cook on low heat 20 minutes or until onion is tender. Then add Worcestershire, catsup, lemon juice, and cayenne pepper. Simmer slowly for 45 minutes. Taste for seasoning. This sauce freezes well.

Yields 4 servings

Recipe from Bully's Best Bites *cookbook, courtesy of the Junior Auxiliary of Starkville, Inc.*

Sweet Treats

KENTUCKY HOSPITALITY BOURBON BALLS

INGREDIENTS:
¼ cup bourbon
2 cups finely chopped pecans
1 cup (2 sticks) butter, softened
1 (5-ounce) can evaporated milk
3 pounds confectioners' sugar
4 cups (24 ounces) semisweet chocolate chips

DIRECTIONS:
Pour the bourbon over the pecans in a bowl and toss to coat. Combine the butter, evaporated milk, and confectioners' sugar in a bowl and blend well. Add the pecan mixture and knead well. Roll into 1-inch balls. Place on a tray and chill until firm.

Temper the chocolate as directed below. Dip the balls into the chocolate using a dipping fork or wooden pick and shake off the excess chocolate. Place on a tray lined with waxed paper. Let stand until cool. Place in individual petite-four packages. (You may substitute 4 cups of candy coating for the semisweet chocolate chips.)

Yields 96 servings

Tempering Chocolate:
To make chocolate suitable for dipping without using paraffin it should be tempered so it will stay glossy and firm at room temperature. Begin by

melting ⅔ of your chocolate to 118°F so it melts, but does not separate. Transfer the chocolate to a second bowl. Gradually add the remaining chocolate, some of it in large lumps, to the melted chocolate. By adding this new "tempered chocolate" it will cool and form the desired crystals needed for decorating and coating. Continue stirring in the pieces until it reaches a temperature of 88°F. Remove any remaining chocolate lumps and reuse to temper another batch of chocolate. At this point, the chocolate is ready to use. Do not allow the chocolate to cool to 77°F or the tempering process will need to be repeated.

Recipe from Pride of Kentucky *cookbook, courtesy University of Kentucky Cooperative Extension Service and Kentucky Department of Agriculture*

FROZEN WHISKEY SOUR

INGREDIENTS:
1 can frozen lemonade concentrate (any size)
1 can bourbon (same size as above)
2 cans water (same size can as frozen lemonade)

DIRECTIONS:
Mix together and put in freezer for 24 hours before serving, as it will take a long time to freeze. Serve in old-fashioned glasses with orange slice and cherry on top. This can be made with gin or vodka. Great summertime drink!

Recipe from Winning Seasons *cookbook, courtesy of the Junior League of Tuscaloosa, Inc.*

DATE BALLS

INGREDIENTS:

¼ cup vegetable oil
½ cup sugar
1 tablespoon lemon juice
1 teaspoon grated lemon rind
½ cup chopped pecans
1 pound pitted dates, chopped
2 cups crisp rice cereal
½ cup confectioners' sugar, sifted

DIRECTIONS:
Pour oil into a large saucepan. Add sugar; stir until well mixed and sugar
partially dissolves. Add lemon juice and rind, pecans, and dates. Mix well.
Add rice cereal, 1 cup at a time, and mix thoroughly. Shape into small
balls; roll in confectioners' sugar. Store in a covered container.

Yields 5 dozen balls. One serving: 2 balls

Recipe from The Auburn Cookbook, *courtesy of the Alabama Cooperative
Extension System (Alabama A&M and Auburn Universities)*

CHEW CAKE

(Favorite of Paul "Bear" Bryant)

INGREDIENTS:
2 eggs, beaten
1 cup flour
1 teaspoon baking powder
½ pound brown sugar
½ stick butter, melted
1 cup nuts, broken

DIRECTIONS:
Preheat over to 350° F. Grease and flour a 9x13-inch pan. Mix eggs with flour, baking powder, brown sugar, and melted butter. Add nuts and spread a thin layer in pan. Bake for 50 minutes. Cool in pan and spread with topping.

TOPPING INGREDIENTS:
¾ cup sugar
½ cup milk
½ stick butter
½ teaspoon vanilla

DIRECTIONS:
Mix sugar, milk, butter, and vanilla. Cook in a heavy saucepan until it forms a soft ball (234°F). Cool, beat until thick, and spread on cake in pan.

Yields 8 to 12 servings

Recipe from Winning Seasons *cookbook, courtesy of the Junior League of Tuscaloosa, Inc*

THE ULTIMATE TAILGATER'S SEC HANDBOOK

PEANUT RAISIN QUICKIES

INGREDIENTS:
1 ½ cups sugar
½ cup corn-oil margarine
¾ cup all-purpose flour
½ cup skim milk
1 ½ cups quick-cooking oats, uncooked
1 teaspoon ground cinnamon
⅔ cup peanut butter
½ cup chopped unsalted dry-roasted peanuts
½ cup chopped raisins
1 cup crushed oat cereal flakes

DIRECTIONS:
Combine the sugar, margarine, flour, and milk in a saucepan and stir until evenly mixed. Cook over medium heat until mixture comes to a full boil. Boil hard for 3 minutes, stirring constantly. Remove from heat and add oats, cinnamon, peanut butter, peanuts, and raisins. Stir well. Spread the oat flakes over a piece of wax paper. Drop dough by teaspoons onto crushed cereal. Roll each drop of dough until coated. Place on wax paper and let stand until cold and firm.

Yields 5 dozen cookies. One serving: 2 cookies

Recipe from The Auburn Cookbook, *courtesy of the Alabama Cooperative Extension System (Alabama A&M and Auburn Universities)*

BOURBON BROWNIES

INGREDIENTS:
¾ cup flour
1 teaspoon baking soda
¼ teaspoon salt
½ cup sugar
⅓ cup margarine
2 tablespoons water
1 cup (6 ounces) chocolate chips
2 eggs
1 teaspoon vanilla extract
1 ½ cup pecan pieces
¼ cup bourbon
White Bourbon Frosting (below)
1 cup (6 ounces) chocolate chips, melted

DIRECTIONS:
Sift the flour, baking soda, and salt into a mixing bowl. Combine the sugar, margarine, and water in a saucepan. Bring to a boil over low heat, stirring constantly. Remove from the heat. Add 1 cup chocolate chips and vanilla and stir until smooth. Add the eggs and beat well. Add to the flour mixture and mix well. Stir in the pecans. Spoon into a greased 9-inch baking pan. Bake at 325°F for 30 to 35 minutes or until the edges pull from the side of the pan. Remove from the oven and pierce holes in the brownies using wooden picks. Pour the bourbon over the top. Let stand until cool. Spread White Bourbon Frosting over the brownies. Spread the melted chocolate chips over the top to glaze.

Yields 12 servings

WHITE BOURBON FROSTING

INGREDIENTS:
¼ cup (½ stick) margarine, softened
2 cups confectioners' sugar
2 tablespoons bourbon
1 tablespoon water

DIRECTIONS:
Beat the margarine, confectioners' sugar, bourbon, and water in a mixing bowl until smooth.

Yields 12 servings

Both recipes from Pride of Kentucky *cookbook, courtesy University of Kentucky Cooperative Extension Service and Kentucky Department of Agriculture*

CHOCOLATE POUND CAKE

INGREDIENTS:
Nonstick vegetable cooking spray
2 tablespoons all-purpose flour
2 ½ cups all-purpose flour
½ cup unsweetened cocoa powder
1 cup corn-oil margarine
2 cups sugar
1 cup brown sugar, firmly packed
6 clean, uncracked eggs
1 teaspoon vanilla
1 teaspoon almond extract
¼ teaspoon baking soda
8 ounces reduced-fat sour cream

DIRECTIONS:
Coat a 10-inch tube pan with cooking spray and dust with 2 tablespoons flour. Combine 2 ½ cups flour and cocoa in a bowl and stir until evenly blended. In a large bowl, cream margarine by beating until soft and smooth. Gradually add both sugars to margarine, beating thoroughly after each addition until light and fluffy. Separate egg whites from yolks. Add yolks, one at a time, to creamed mixture, beating thoroughly after each addition. Add vanilla and almond and stir until well blended. In a small bowl, combine baking soda and sour cream and beat until it is well blended. Add the flour mixture and sour cream mixture alternately to the creamed mixture by adding ⅓ of the flour and ½ of the sour cream at a time, beginning and ending with the flour. Beat on low speed after each addition until well blended. Then beat at medium speed for 2 minutes. Beat the 6 egg whites until stiff but still moist looking. Add egg whites to batter and fold in by cutting a spoon through egg whites and batter and

turning batter over egg whites. Continue doing this until they are thoroughly blended and no egg whites are visible. Do not beat or stir. Pour batter evenly into pan. Bake at 325°F for 1 ½ hours or until done. Cool in pan on wire rack for 10 minutes. Remove cake from pan and finish cooling on rack. You can dust with confectioners' sugar, drizzle with glaze, or serve plain. To serve, cut into 1-inch wedges.

Yields 32 servings

Recipe from The Auburn Cookbook, *Alabama Cooperative Extension System (Alabama A&M and Auburn Universities), revised 1996. Used by permission. All rights reserved.*

ALMOND BALL

INGREDIENTS:
¼ gallon vanilla ice cream
3 (3 ½-ounce) packages toasted sliced almonds
Hot fudge sauce

DIRECTIONS:
Divide ice cream into 8 equal portions and form into balls. Roll in almonds. Pour hot fudge sauce over each ball and serve.

Yields 8 servings

Recipe from Winning Seasons *cookbook, courtesy of the Junior League of Tuscaloosa, Inc*

RESOURCES

Before you head to the car, you may need to find the best place to get more information on throwing a great tailgate party, or where to find the stuff with which to do it. Of course, you'll find tailgating tips (including game-day and travel checklists), podcasts, videos, and recipes at both **theultimatetailgater.com** and **theultimatetailgatechef.com**, but there are also a number of other sources to help grow your tailgating knowledge.

You can find all sorts of helpful tools and information about tailgating from the **American Tailgaters Association** at atatailgate.com. The ATA is a national organization that promotes tailgating, offers members discounts on tailgating supplies and gear, reviews tailgating products, and more. I'm thrilled they endorse The Ultimate Tailgater books. Membership is free, and you can sign up online.

If you're looking for help getting tickets or finding a place to stay in any SEC city, **FanHub** can hook you up. They work with ticket brokers and hotel room wholesalers to find the best deals for traveling fans. They also have fan forums so you can learn more about the stadium and things to do in town, as well as pipe in with your own experiences and thoughts. You'll find it all at fanhub.com.

Of course, you'll also need tailgating gear if you want to do things like sit and eat. Don't worry, I'm here for you. From grills to frilly hats (be careful who you let see you wearing the frilly hat), there are thousands of resources online if you can't find anything in stores near you.

Grills & Accessories

Before buying it's a good idea to compare features and options to make sure you get the best grill for your style of tailgating. Some good sources of information and research are:

bbq.about.com/od/grills/index.htm?terms=grills
consumersearch.com/www/sports_and_leisure/gas-grill-reviews/index.html

With your newfound grill knowledge, you're ready to get your grill. Here are some sites for tailgating grills and accessories:

bbqgalore.com
brinkmann.net
campchef.com
campingworld.com
ducane.com
freedomgrill.com
grillingaccessories.com
grilllovers.com
homedepot.com
lowes.com
webergrills.com

Tents

All across the SEC you'll find a sea of tents outside the stadium. There are so many in places like The Grove that I'm not sure the ground would get wet if it rained. For many tailgaters a canopy is enough. But for others, tents with sides and other options make for the ultimate tailgate party. You can find a variety of tents on these Web sites:

canopycenter.com
elitedeals.com/nctatelocate.html
eurekatents.com
ezupdirect.com
kdkanopy.com
shopping.com/xGS-Tailgating_Tents

General Tailgating Supplies

From licensed products to coolers to tables to chairs to . . . you get the idea.

americantailgater.com
collegegear.com
footballfanatics.com
tailgatehq.com
tailgatepartyshop.com
tailgatetown.com
tailgatingsupplies.com

Party Decorations

To turn your parking spot into a parking lot party you need to dress it up. In addition to food, drinks, and friends, party lights, banners, and pompoms help.

4funparties.com
bulkpartysupplies.com
party411.com
partyoptions.net/party_supply/football-main-page.htm
partypro.com
partyshelf.com/football.htm

SEC Schools and Teams

If you'd like to learn more about any of the 12 SEC schools and their athletic programs, you can visit these official sites. Many of the athletic sites also have links to additional statistics and news.

SCHOOL SITES

Alabama:	ua.edu
Arkansas:	uark.edu
Auburn:	auburn.edu
Florida:	ufl.edu
Georgia:	uga.edu
Kentucky:	uky.edu
LSU:	lsu.edu

Ole Miss:	olemiss.edu
Mississippi State:	msstate.edu
South Carolina:	sc.edu
Tennessee:	utk.edu
Vanderbilt:	vanderbilt.edu

ATHLETIC SITES

Alabama:	RollTide.com
Arkansas:	hogwired.com
Auburn:	auburntigers.cstv.com
Florida:	gatorzone.com
Georgia:	georgiadogs.com
Kentucky:	ukathletics.com
LSU:	LSUsports.com
Ole Miss:	olemisssports.com
Mississippi State:	mstateathletics.com
South Carolina:	uscsports.cstv.com
Tennessee:	utsports.com
Vanderbilt:	vucommodores.cstv.com

ALUMNI ASSOCIATION SITES

Alabama:	alumni.ua.edu
Arkansas:	alumni.uark.edu
Auburn:	aualum.org
Florida:	ufalumni.ufl.edu
Georgia:	alumni.uga.edu/alumni
Kentucky:	ukalumni.net
LSU:	lsualumni.org
Ole Miss:	alumni.olemiss.edu
Mississippi State:	alumni.msstate.edu
South Carolina:	carolinaalumni.org
Tennessee:	utalumni.utk.edu
Vanderbilt:	vanderbilt.edu/alumni

Also by Stephen Linn

FOX Sports Tailgating Handbook
The Ultimate Tailgater's ACC Handbook
The Ultimate Tailgater's Big 12 Handbook
The Ultimate Tailgater's Big Ten Handbook
The Ultimate Tailgater's Pac-10 Handbook
The Ultimate Tailgater's Handbook
The Ultimate Tailgater's Travel Guide
The Ultimate Tailgater's Racing Guide

Available in stores and at **theultimatetailgater.com.**

Also on **theultimatetailgater.com** you'll find tailgating videos, podcasts, recipes, contests, and more!

For everything you need to know about the centerpiece of your tailgate party—the food—visit theultimatetailgatechef.com! There you'll find cooking videos, podcasts, recipes, tips, and more!